Learning in Europe

The ERASMUS Experience

Higher Education Policy Series 14
ERASMUS Monograph No. 14

Learning in Europe

The ERASMUS Experience

A Survey of the 1988-89 ERASMUS Students

Friedhelm Maiworm, Wolfgang Steube
and Ulrich Teichler

Jessica Kingsley Publishers, London

ERASMUS Bureau, Brussels

First published in the United Kingdom in 1991 by
Jessica Kingsley Publishers Ltd
118 Pentonville Road
London N1 9JN

Copyright © 1991 Friedhelm Maiworm, Wolfgang Steube and Ulrich Teichler

The present report has been prepared in the context of the monitoring and evaluation of the European Community Action Scheme for the Mobility of University Students (ERASMUS). It is designed primarily for use within the services of the Commission of the European Communities, and although the report is being placed at the disposal of the general public, it is emphasized that the views which it contains are those of the authors and do not necessarily represent the official position of the Commission or of the ERASMUS Bureau, which assists the Commission in the management of ERASMUS.

British Library Cataloguing in Publication Data
Maiworm, Friedhelm
    Learning in Europe: the ERASMUS experience:
    A survey of the 1988-89 ERASMUS students.
    - (Higher education policy series)
    I. Title II. Steube, Wolfgang
    III. Teichler, Ulrich IV. Series
    378.4

    ISBN 1-85302-527-5
    ISSN 0954-3716

Printed and bound in Great Britain by
Biddles Ltd, Guildford and King's Lynn

Content

Preface

The European Community Action Scheme for the Mobility of University Students (ERASMUS) was established by the Council Decision of 15 June 1987. The first phase of the Programme covered the academic years 1987/88 - 1989/90, the second phase being based on the amended Council Decision of 14 December 1989. The Programme is open to all types of higher education institutions and all subject areas.

The central element of the ERASMUS Programme is the furthering of student mobility within the European Community. The student mobility programmes established under the Programme offer university students a chance to undertake a substantial period of study (minimum 3 months) in another Community Member State fully recognized by the home institution as an integral part of their degree. The Inter-University Cooperation Programmes (ICPs) set up under ERASMUS can incorporate (in addition to the student mobility programmes mentioned above) other activities such as teaching staff mobility, development of new joint curricula, and intensive programmes. Collectively, the ICPs constitute the European University Network established under ERASMUS.

In 1989, the European Community Course Credit Transfer System (ECTS) was introduced as an experimental pilot project designed to test the European potential of credit transfer as an effective means of academic recognition.

Furthermore, ERASMUS offers the possibility to all university staff members of undertaking preparatory visits, study visits or teaching visits to other universities within the Community, and provides support for a wide range of complementary activities seeking to improve the climate for academic exchange and cooperation within the Community.

Since the inception of ERASMUS, great importance has been attached to ensure a thorough evaluation of the Programme's progress. The Task Force Human Resources, Education, Training and Youth of the Commission of the European Communities has therefore commissioned or supported the preparation of a number of studies on various aspects of the Programme's development.

These studies, though designed primarily for use within the services of the Commission of the European Communities, are now being published in the ERASMUS Monograph series, in order to make them accessible to a wider public. The studies are all based on the fairly limited material available in the first years of the Programme, and they are of varying length and quality, but each in its own way contributes to the overall evaluation process of the Programme in more than just a historical sense. The evaluations of academic recognition matters, of the development of specific subject areas, of the role of language training, of accommodation matters etc. are all of relevance to anyone working with and having an interest in ERASMUS. The full list of studies appears elsewhere in the present volume.

It is emphasized that the views which the present study contains are those of the author and do not necessarily represent the official position of the Commission or of the ERASMUS Bureau, which assists the Commission in the management of ERASMUS.

Chapter 1

Introduction

In 1987, the Commission of the European Community inaugurated an Action Scheme for the Mobility of University Students (ERASMUS). The long-term objective of the ERASMUS programme is to have enabled 10 percent of the students at higher education institutions in Europe to spend a period of study in another EC Member State.

The ERASMUS programme provides support for various activities. Undoubtedly the most visible one, involving large numbers of students each year, is the provision of grants for students spending a study period of between three months to a full academic year in another country of the European Community. The grants are supplementary, aiming to bear, in principle, the costs for travel to and from the host country as well as additional costs abroad. They are predominantly awarded to students taking part in Inter-University Cooperation Programmes (ICPs), where two or more university departments in different EC Member States cooperate in the provision for regular exchange of students. ICPs as a rule incorporate various administrative and educational measures to ease the success of exchange, and aim to secure (at least to some extent) the recognition of study achievements abroad upon return by the home institution of higher education. In addition, some students, who are individually mobile, i.e. outside the framework of such programmes, are awarded ERASMUS grants in certain Member States.

In 1988/89, the second year of the ERASMUS programme, awards for supplementary grants were made to 942 ICPs, aimed to support about 16 000 students[1]. In the event, just over 11 000 students (as compared to about 4 000 students in 1987/88) went to another EC

---

1   Commission of the European Communities. ERASMUS: *Directory of Programmes 1988/89*. Brussels and Luxembourg: Office for Official Publications of the European Communities, 1989.

Member State with the support of an EC mobility grant[2].

From the outset of the ERASMUS programme, efforts have been made to evaluate both the processes and outcomes of student mobility supported by the ERASMUS programme as well as the provisions of the scheme and their impacts. A first report aiming to summarize the experiences acquired was published by the Commission in December 1989[3]. This report, which formed the basis for the decisions underlying the extension of the ERASMUS programme beyond its inaugural period from 1987 to 1990, was based on preliminary statistics, first-hand experiences, and small surveys.

In 1989, the Commission decided to support a project aiming to analyse the experiences of a large number of ERASMUS students. A survey was conducted to provide useful information for future students opting for a study period in another EC Member State, and feedback for institutions of higher education and their departments participating in the activities aiming to support student mobility. It also provided a basis for evaluation and reconsideration of the scheme on the part of the Commission of the European Communities and the various persons and agencies involved in the decision-making and administration of the scheme on institutional, national and supra-national levels.

The study is based on replies to a written questionnaire by 3 212 students who undertook a study period abroad in 1988/89 with the help of an ERASMUS grant. The study, conducted a few months after the beginning of the subsequent academic year, provides information on the participating students, their preparation for their sojourn, how they lived and studied in the host country and what supportive provisions had been made by the home and host universities. It also provides statistics on their financial resources and expenses, their perception of the academic, cultural and foreign language impact of the study period abroad, their general assessments of the scheme and finally the degree of recognition granted by their home institutions on return. In addition to this general range of themes, special emphasis was placed on issues of accommodation - a topic hotly debated at the time the survey was

---

2   See U. Teichler, R. Kreitz and F. Maiworm. *Student Mobility within ERASMUS 1988/89*. Kassel Wissenschaftliches Zentrum für Berufs- und Hochschulforschung, 1991; ERASMUS Monographs, No. 12.

3   Commission of the European Communities. ERASMUS Programme: Report on the Experience Acquired in the Application of the ERASMUS Programme 1987-1989. Brussels, 13 December 1989 (SEC(89) 2051), mimeo.

conducted. Underlying concepts and questions raised will be explained in respective chapters of this publication.

The concepts as well as the methodology of the study were largely based on the experiences acquired in the framework of a large-scale evaluation project on various types of study abroad programmes and various support schemes, including the Joint Study Programmes (the support scheme by the Commission of the European Communities preceding the ERASMUS programme). The results of this project, the preliminary reports of which fed into the decision-making process regarding the inauguration of the ERASMUS programmes in 1986 and 1987, were recently published in two volumes[4]. A substantial part of the questions posed to the ERASMUS students mirrored those asked in the mid-eighties to various students in the United Kingdom, France, the Federal Republic of Germany, Sweden and the US. This approach not only eased the preparation of this project, but also provided a basis for comparison of results. A few questions regarding accommodation were similarly phrased to those by R. Hughes[5].

The study was conducted at the Centre for Research on Higher Education and Work of the Comprehensive University of Kassel (Federal Republic of Germany). The research team was headed by Ulrich Teichler, who participated in the above mentioned research project on various study abroad programmes and support schemes. Friedhelm Maiworm, Wolfgang Steube and Ulrich Teichler conducted the study and wrote this report. Kristin Gagelmann took over many responsibilities in administering the survey as well as the processing of this text. Students from the various EC Member States enrolled at the Comprehensive University of Kassel helped in the analysis of the responses and the data processing. The study was eased by substantial support from the ERASMUS Bureau, notably from Alan Smith, Inge Knudsen, Irene Magill, Anthony Smallwood and Lesley Wilson. Persons in charge of coordinating the student mobility at the various departments provided the students' addresses. Many experts in charge of academic or administrative issues of ERASMUS programmes in various Member States of the European Community provided valuable

---

4   B.B. Burn, L. Cerych and A. Smith, eds. Study Abroad Programmes. London: Jessica Kingsley, 1990; S. Opper, U. Teichler and J. Carlson. *The Impacts of Study Abroad Programmes on Students and Graduates*. London: Jessica Kingsley, 1990.

5   *Homes Far from Home*. London: Overseas Students Trust, 1990.

advice and support for all stages of the project. Last but not least, the 3 212 students who each spent more than one hour in completing the questionnaire were the key persons in ensuring a set of comprehensive and interesting findings on the experiences of the ERASMUS students.

Chapter 2

Research Design, Methods and Procedures

This study is based on the questionnaire survey "Experiences of ERASMUS Students 1988/89", the preparation of which began in summer 1989. Experiences acquired in a previous survey of students participating in various kinds of study abroad programmes (cf. Chapter 1) and meetings with experts from the Commission of the European Community, the ERASMUS Bureau, persons involved in the ERASMUS network and other experts helped in setting thematic priorities and in formulating the questionnaire.

Students were asked to provide information regarding:
- their biography and educational careers
- the patterns of the ERASMUS supported period
- preparation for the study abroad period
- advice and support provided by the host university
- living in the host country
- studying at the host university
- accommodation
- financial resources and expenses
- foreign language proficiency before and after the study period abroad
- knowledge of and opinion about the host country culture and society
- academic achievements and recognition of study abroad
- summarizing assessment of the life and study period in the host country.

The questionnaire comprised 16 pages, more than 50 questions and about 650 variables. Most of the questions were closed, though leaving room for statements in a final open category "others". At the end of the questionnaire, students were asked to describe their worst and best experiences as well as difficulties successfully overcome. The questionnaire was translated into eight of the nine official EC languages. Greek students were sent questionnaires in both English and French, because the translation was not completed in time. Students in Belgium were given a questionnaire in both French and Dutch.

Programme administrators at the individual universities were asked in the summer of 1989 to provide addresses of the students of the ERASMUS programme. This resulted in about 5 031 addresses - the addresses of about half of the participating students and as mailing to about 4 000 students was originally envisaged in order to ensure at least 2 000 responses, the questionnaire was sent to all available addresses. The survey did not include the individually mobile students supported by the ERASMUS programme (free movers), as addresses of these students, who comprised less than ten percent of all ERASMUS students in 1988/89, were not yet available at the time the survey was conducted.

The survey was conducted at the time when all students had not only completed the study period in the host country, but also had experienced life and study at the home institution again - even in some cases received recognition for their study abroad achievements - and thus could view it from a full range of perspectives. During the third week of November 1989, all ERASMUS students for whom addresses were available, were sent the questionnaire by the ERASMUS Bureau. The front page of the questionnaire contained a short address by the Director of the ERASMUS Bureau, explaining the rationale of the study and asking for information, as well as a note from the head of the research project, explaining the survey measures taken to assure confidentiality. Finally, major terms used in the study were explained on the front pages, including the fact that the term "university" refers to all institutions recognized as institutions of higher education in the EC Member States. A return envelope and postage stamps were provided.

Chart 2.1 shows the timing of responses with almost 400 questionnaires received during the third week after the first mailing. The pattern of weekly responses over a period of four months was interrupted by two further peaks of return due to the Christmas and New Year vacations and the reminder letter which was sent out in mid January to non-responders.

Chart 2.1
Return of the Questionnaires

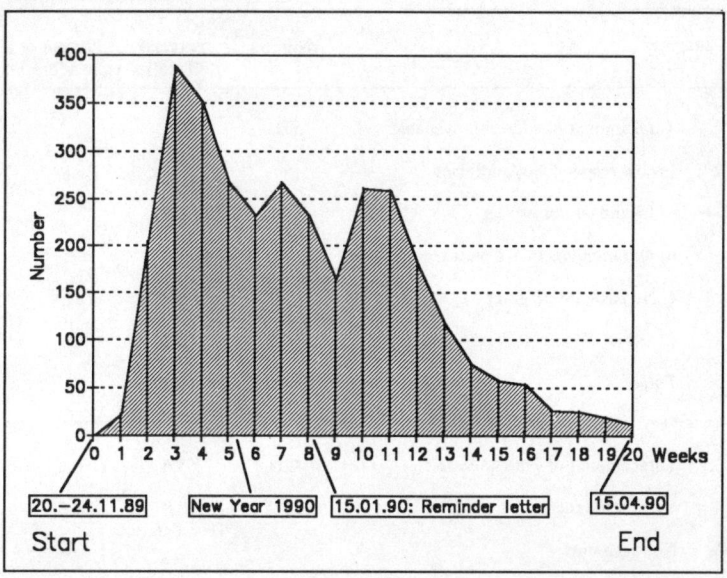

Of the 5 031 questionnaires, 95 (1.9 %) were returned because the addresses were not valid. Of the remaining 4 936 questionnaires, 3 337 (67.6 %) were returned, in most cases with responses to the questions and in a few cases merely by letters. Over 120 of the responses had to be excluded, for reasons ranging from non receipt of grants, or staying abroad for less than four weeks (and hence more likely to have received support in the framework of Intensive Programmes), or exceptionally for a study period outside the European Community. Finally, out of a total number of 4 811 valid addresses, 3 212 valid responses were received (see the overview in Table 2.1) within 20 weeks (a few late responses could not be taken into consideration). The high response rate of 66.8 percent indicates that the questionnaire was well received by most ERASMUS students who were willing to provide feedback of their experience which might be useful to further generations of students, persons in charge of exchange programmes and to those politically and administratively responsible for the ERASMUS programme in general.

Table 2.1
Return Rate of ERASMUS-Survey 1988/98

Category	Number	Percent (Total)	Percent of valid addresses
1. Total amount of addresses available	5031	100.0	
2. Invalid respondents/addresses:			
a) Invalid addresses	95	1.9	
b) Duration less than 4 weeks	70	1.4	
c) No ERASMUS grant	46	0.9	
d) Other	9	0.2	
Total	220	4.4	
3. Total amount of valid addresses	4811	95.6	100.0
4. Valid respondents	3212	63.8	66.8
5. Non-response			
a) Questionnaires not sent back	1579	31.4	32.8
b) Blank questionnaires (sent back without any comment)	20	0.4	0.4

Both the rates of provisions of addresses and the return rates of questionnaires mailed (for the latter see Table 2.2) varied according to the home country. As the statistical overview on the 1988/89 ERASMUS students provides some profile data which had been asked in the questionnaire as well, it is possible to examine the extent to which the 3 212 responses are representative of almost all of the 1988/89 ERASMUS students. A few French universities did not provide information for the statistical analysis and hence the rates of students surveyed among all ERASMUS students presented in Table 2.2 are not exact.

Table 2.2
Representation of ERASMUS Students in the Survey and Return Rate by Country of Home University

Country of home university	A All ERASMUS students* Number	A %	B Valid adress Number	B %	C Respondents provided Number	C %	Representation ratio (C : A)	Return rate (C : B)
B	403	4.1	280	5.8	216	6.7	53.6	77.1
D	1,715	17.2	1072	22.2	801	24.9	46.7	74.7
DK	187	1.9	58	1.2	44	1.4	23.5	75.8
E	1,064	10.7	500	10.4	312	9.7	29.3	62.4
F	1,779	17.9	966	20.1	673	21.0	37.8	69.6
G	194	2.0	67	1.4	37	1.2	19.1	55.2
I	1,390	14.0	446	9.3	285	8.9	20.5	63.9
IRL	193	1.9	93	1.9	41	1.3	21.2	44.0
NL	664	6.7	266	5.5	156	4.9	23.5	58.6
P	161	1.6	17	.4	10	.3	6.2	58.8
UK	2,164	21.8	1046	21.7	637	19.8	29.4	60.8
Total	9914	100.0	4811	100.0	3212	100	32.4	66.8

* We estimate that this figure represents 90 % of the participating students (according to information available at the ERASMUS Bureau in March 1991, the total number of students awarded ERASMUS grants in 1988/89 was 11,228).

According to the available data, the survey covered a range from 54 percent of all Belgian and 47 percent of all German ERASMUS students to only 19 percent of Greek ERASMUS students. The rate of Portuguese students represented in the survey was a low six percent, because very few Portuguese university departments provided addresses. In addition, students from Luxembourg were not included at all, since all of them were 'free movers' who were omitted from this study.

The representation rate varied considerably by host country, subject and length of stay: for example the host country rate ranged from 40 percent of students going to Greece to 29 percent of those going to Denmark. Students enrolled in engineering (43 %) and business studies (42 %) were overrepresented among respondents and, finally, 38 percent of those going abroad for more than six months were represented in the survey, compared with 28 percent going abroad for less than this period.

In order to control the possible impact of the overrepresentation and underrepresentation according to major profile data, corrected survey data were produced in which the frequency distribution of the survey data was statistically adjusted to all 1988/89 ERASMUS students according to country of home institution, host country, field of study, and duration of the study period abroad. However, as recognition of study abroad turned out to be only marginally lower in the corrected data set than among all students surveyed (see Chapter 8), the subsequent analysis is based on the uncorrected data set, i.e. all students responding.

Formal checks of the responses and the coding of open questions were taken care of by members of the research team with the aid of students from the respective countries. The data processing and statistical analysis took place on the Siemens BS2000 computer at the Comprehensive University of Kassel and on IBM personal computers at the Centre for Research on Higher Education and Work. Programme packages SPSS-X served the statistical analysis and the provision of tables.

Chapter 3

The Participating Students

3.1 Purpose of the Overview

Some basic data asked for in the questionnaire, i.e. country of home university, country of host university, field of study, age, years of study prior to the study period abroad, and finally the duration of the study period, were made available to almost all students by the participating universities and are documented in another publication. Such data allowed us to examine to what extent the composition of the respondents corresponded with that of all students who were supported by the ERASMUS programme, and thus show the extent to which the respondents were representative of all ERASMUS students (see Chapter 2). Further biographical data were surveyed, such as nationality, sex, parents' educational background, prior educational and work experience, prior stays abroad, changes of field of study, and family status. All data presented in this Chapter serve as reference data for the subsequent analysis: What is the composition of the students responding to the questionnaire in terms of fields, duration of study in the host country, prior education, etc.? In some cases, reference will be made to differences between the composition of respondents and that of the "population", i.e. all 1988/89 ERASMUS students.

3.1 Nationality, Home Country and Host Country

For convenience sake, we talk of "British", "French", "Spanish" students etc. in the subsequent text if we refer to the country of the home institution of higher education; we do so because all major issues of this study refer to contrasts or cooperation between partner institutions of higher education from the respective countries. One should bear in

mind, though, that three percent of the ERASMUS students were foreigners, i.e. not citizens of the country of the home institution of higher education. The quota of foreign students was:
- seven percent at universities in the United Kingdom
- five percent at universities in Ireland
- four percent at universities in France
- three percent at universities in the Federal Republic of Germany
- two percent at universities in Belgium
- one percent or less in the remaining six countries.

The largest proportion of foreign students were Irish students in the United Kingdom and British students in Ireland; otherwise, the nationalities of foreign students in the respective (home) countries were widely spread.

The distribution of students according to home country was already referred to in Chapter 2, when the rates of return and representation were discussed (see Table 2.2). A detailed overview is provided in Table 3.1. Two thirds of the ERASMUS students responding studied prior to their sojourn in the "large" countries: The Federal Republic of Germany (25 %), France (21 %) and the United Kingdom (20 %). Spain (10 %), Italy (9 %), Belgium (7 %) and the Netherlands (5 %) could be named "medium size" countries as far as the absolute number of ERASMUS students were concerned, whereas altogether about five percent of the students surveyed were from Denmark, Ireland, Greece and Portugal.

Major host countries of the ERASMUS students surveyed were the United Kingdom (30 %) and France (26 %), whereas only 12 percent of the students went to Germany. The participating British universities hosted 1.5 times as many students surveyed as they sent, whereas German universities hosted less than half the number of students surveyed as they sent abroad. These "imbalances" visible among the respondents, however, are substantially smaller among all ERASMUS students.

Spain (10 %), Italy (7 %) and the Netherlands (6 %) were not infrequent hosts either; for example, Italy hosted two-thirds of the number of students they sent abroad, compared with Belgium who hosted only three percent of all the ERASMUS students surveyed, i.e. less than half of the number of the students they sent abroad. Finally, three percent of surveyed students went to Ireland and one percent each to Greece, Portugal and Denmark; Ireland and Portugal clearly hosted more students than they sent abroad.

Although it should be stressed that these figures refer to the students responding to the questionnaire, their distribution by host country hardly differs from that of all ERASMUS students in 1988/89. Only students going to the United Kingdom were somewhat overrepresented among the respondents (30 % in the survey as compared to 28 % among all ERASMUS students), whereas those going to Germany were underrepresented (12 % as compared to 15 %).

Table 3.1
Country of Home University and Host Country (absolute numbers)

Country of home university	Host country											Total
	B	D	DK	E	F	GR	I	IRL	NL	P	UK	
B	0	12	1	24	62	0	13	9	68	1	26	216
D	6	0	1	92	227	4	39	45	28	7	352	801
DK	0	5	0	0	8	1	3	8	4	0	15	44
E	17	35	4	0	135	11	25	9	8	1	67	312
F	10	137	1	89	0	9	25	17	14	14	357	673
GR	0	8	4	0	5	0	3	0	1	0	16	37
I	13	42	0	34	73	9	0	8	18	5	83	285
IRL	5	6	0	2	10	0	6	0	1	1	10	41
NL	26	25	10	19	10	2	18	9	0	2	35	156
P	0	0	0	4	2	0	2	2	0	0	0	10
UK	17	101	11	50	317	7	76	2	46	10	0	637
Total	94	371	32	314	849	43	210	109	188	41	961	3212

In looking at the "flows" from home to host countries, we note that 46 percent of the students surveyed were exchanged among the United Kingdom, France and Germany, a further 40 percent of the flows between these three countries and the other EC Member States, and 14 percent among the other EC Member States. As compared to these survey data, statistics of all ERASMUS students show that 40 percent were exchanged between the United Kingdom, France and Germany, and 46 percent between these three and the other countries. The proportion of those exchanged between the other countries among all ERASMUS (14 %) did not differ from the respective proportion among the respondents.

It should be noted that the Commission pursues a deliberate policy of stimulating the increased involvement of small EC Member States and Member States with less common languages. According to estimates by the Commission, the proportion of ERASMUS student mobility among the three major countries declined from 62 percent in 1987/88 to 48 percent in 1988/89 and eventually to 42 percent in 1989/90. On the other hand, the proportion of exchange among the remaining EC Member States increased during the same period from eight percent to ten percent in the year surveyed, and eventually to 12 percent in the subsequent year[1]. We note some clusters of exchange:

- as regards exchange between two countries in both directions, overproportional mobility can be observed between Belgium and the Netherlands, Denmark and the Netherlands, and between Greece and the United Kingdom
- overproportional mobility is also visible within the triangle of British, French and German institutions of higher education
- a relatively strong "influx" might be observed at Italian universities from students from the Netherlands and the United Kingdom, among Irish institutions from students from the Federal Republic of Germany, the Netherlands and Denmark, and finally at Portuguese institutions from students from France.

3.2   Fields of Study

The largest proportion of ERASMUS students surveyed were enrolled in business studies (33 %) during the period abroad, followed by foreign language studies (18 %), law (11 %) and engineering (10 %). Altogether

---

[1]   Commission of the European Communities. ERASMUS Programme: Report on the Experience Acquired in the Application of the ERASMUS Programme 1987-1989. Brussels, 1989, mimeo.

a total of 28 percent, less than one to four percent each, were represented in the remaining fields of study or groups of fields presented in Table 3.2.

There were some interesting differences in participation rates across countries and subjects: many British and German ERASMUS students were enrolled in business studies, while law was strongly represented among Greek, Belgian and Dutch students. Many Danish ERASMUS students were enrolled in engineering, and many Spanish students in foreign language studies.

There was quite a spread of host countries chosen by ERASMUS students from the respective fields. Some overrepresentations, however, deserve attention. Students in engineering and business most frequently opted for one of the three "large" countries while students in architecture and humanities most often went to other countries (in the former case frequently to Spain and Portugal and also overproportionally to Italy and the Netherlands, and in the latter case to Spain, Italy and the Netherlands).

Altogether, nine percent of the ERASMUS students named different major fields of study prior to the study abroad period from the one they were enrolled in while abroad. On the other hand, six percent of the ERASMUS students moved to a different field when returning to the home institution from the one in which they were enrolled abroad. In many cases, a lack of a clear match of fields or a slightly different categorisation of fields between the partner institutions might explain these shifts. Therefore, the most interesting information is the level of change between fields from study prior to and after the study period abroad. As Table 3.3 shows, seven percent of the ERASMUS students returned afterwards to a different field of study in their home institutions from the one they were enrolled in prior to the study abroad period.

It might be added that seven percent of students surveyed had changed their field of study already prior to the period abroad - they had studied on average 1.3 years in other fields before they changed to the field they were enrolled in prior to the study abroad period. This was most often reported by French students (14 %) - obviously the French structure of a two-year first cycle eased transfers. On the other hand, change of fields prior to the study abroad period were rare among Portuguese, Spanish, Greek and British students.

Table 3.2
Major Field of Study During Study Period Abroad, by Country of Home University (percentage)

	Country of home university											Total
	B	D	DK	E	F	GR	I	IRL	NL	P	UK	
Agricultural sciences	0	0	0	2	1	3	0	0	7	0	1	1
Architect., urb./reg. plann.	4	2	7	1	2	0	14	7	0	0	3	3
Art and design	2	2	0	2	0	0	1	2	6	0	2	2
Business/management sc.	13	42	28	21	35	14	24	20	12	80	43	33
Education, teacher training	1	2	0	1	0	5	1	0	1	0	0	1
Engineering, technology	10	12	37	6	18	14	2	10	1	0	4	10
Geography, geology	0	0	0	3	0	3	1	7	1	0	0	1
Humanities	5	3	0	8	1	0	5	2	1	0	4	4
Lang., philological sc.	11	16	0	33	19	0	15	12	9	0	22	18
Law	30	10	0	8	9	38	9	5	28	0	5	11
Mathematics, informatics	3	2	0	4	2	0	5	0	3	0	1	2
Medical sciences	3	1	2	2	1	8	2	0	0	0	1	1
Natural sciences	2	4	7	3	4	8	4	22	1	20	1	4
Social sciences	5	2	16	3	2	3	8	5	14	0	3	4
Comm./information sc.	2	0	0	0	0	5	1	2	1	0	0	0
Other areas of study	9	0	2	3	5	0	9	5	11	0	7	5
Total	100	100	100	100	100	100	100	100	100	100	100	100
(n)	(215)	(801)	(43)	(312)	(672)	(37)	(285)	(41)	(156)	(10)	(637)	(3209)

Question 2.3: Please state your major field of study and tick the respective group of fields: b. during the study period abroad.

Table 3.3
Major Field of Study Before Study Period Abroad, by Field of Study After Study Period Abroad (absolute numbers)

	Major field - after study period abroad																Total
	I	II	III	IV	V	VI	VII	VIII	IX	X	XI	XII	XIII	XIV	XV	XVI	
Agricultural sciences	33	2	0	1	0	0	0	0	0	0	0	0	0	0	0	1	37
Architecture, urban and regional planning	0	95	1	0	0	0	0	0	0	0	0	0	0	0	0	1	97
Art and design	0	0	47	0	0	0	0	1	0	0	0	0	0	0	0	0	48
Business studies, management sciences	0	0	0	934	0	4	0	0	11	2	1	0	0	1	0	11	964
Education, teacher training	0	0	0	1	40	0	0	0	7	0	0	0	0	0	0	0	48
Engineering, technology	0	2	0	9	2	292	0	0	0	0	7	0	2	0	0	3	317
Geography, geology	0	2	0	1	0	0	19	0	0	0	0	0	1	0	0	1	24
Humanities	0	0	1	3	0	0	0	93	6	2	0	0	0	3	0	0	108
Languages, philological sciences	0	0	1	10	1	0	1	13	526	6	1	0	0	5	3	8	575
Law	0	0	0	5	1	0	0	1	3	315	0	0	0	2	1	4	332

(Table 3.3 to be cont.)

(Table 3.3 cont.)

Major field - after study period abroad

	I	II	III	IV	V	VI	VII	VIII	IX	X	XI	XII	XIII	XIV	XV	XVI	Total
Mathematics, informatics	0	0	0	2	0	1	0	1	1	0	66	0	0	0	2	3	76
Medical sciences	0	0	0	0	0	0	0	0	0	0	0	45	0	0	0	0	45
Natural sciences	0	0	0	3	0	4	2	0	0	0	1	1	131	0	0	2	144
Social Sciences	0	0	0	2	0	0	0	1	3	1	0	0	0	116	0	2	125
Communication and information sciences	0	0	0	1	0	1	0	1	0	0	0	0	0	0	9	1	13
Other areas of study	0	0	1	9	0	0	0	1	2	2	3	1	1	3	0	117	140
Total	33	101	51	981	44	302	22	112	559	328	79	47	135	130	15	154	3093

I   = Agricultural sciences
II   = Architecture, urban and regional planning
III = Art and design
IV   = Business studies, management sciences
V   = Education, teacher training
VI   = Engineering, technology
VII = Geography, geology
VIII = Humanities

IX   = Languages, philological sciences
X   = Law
XI   = Mathematics, informatics
XII = Medical sciences
XIII = Natural sciences
XIV = Social Sciences
XV   = Communication and information sciences
XVI = Other areas of study

Question 2.3: Please state your major field of study and tick the respective group of fields: a. immediately before the study period abroad, c. after the study period abroad (if different from a.)

3.3 Age and Previous Study

57 percent of the ERASMUS students surveyed were 21-23 years old in 1989, i.e. at the end of the study period abroad with only 13 percent older than 25, and an average reported age of 23.4 years. As Table 3.4 shows, most French (22.3 years on average) and British students (22.4 years) were relatively young, whereas Danish (25.4 years), German, Greek (24.4 years each) and Dutch (24.2 years) were eldest on average.

Female ERASMUS students surveyed were on average 23.0 years old in 1989 as compared to 23.8 years for the male students. This difference was largely due, as shown below, to the fact that male students spent more time outside general educational careers, for example in military service, employment and vocational training.

Table 3.4
Age at Time of Study Abroad, by Country of Home University (percentage)

	B	D	DK	E	F	GR	I	IRL	NL	P	UK	Total
18	0	0	0	0	0	0	0	0	0	0	0	0
19	0	0	0	3	2	0	0	2	0	0	2	1
20	0	1	0	3	8	0	6	10	1	0	13	6
21	4	4	0	6	21	8	9	20	5	10	35	15
22	13	11	5	22	31	19	20	20	16	10	24	20
23	47	23	11	29	21	17	19	20	28	30	9	22
24	21	19	25	17	9	17	13	10	21	30	5	14
25	8	15	16	9	4	11	13	5	12	0	2	9
26	3	12	23	5	2	6	6	7	7	0	1	6
27	1	7	9	2	1	8	3	0	1	10	1	3
28	1	4	2	1	0	8	2	2	2	10	2	2
29	0	2	2	1	0	0	3	0	1	0	0	1
30	0	1	2	0	0	3	2	2	2	0	1	1
More than 30 years	0	1	5	1	1	3	4	2	4	0	4	2
Total	100	100	100	100	100	100	100	100	100	100	100	100
(n)	(213)	(796)	(44)	(310)	(668)	(36)	(283)	(41)	(156)	(10)	(628)	(3185)

The differences in the age at the time of the study abroad period, in addition to age at the time of first enrolment, reflected to some extent the timing of the study abroad period in the course of study. As Table 3.5 shows, 32 percent spent their study period abroad during the third year of study, with the fourth and fifth year of study the next most frequent options (18 % and 16 %). 12 percent went abroad during their second year of study, and 11 percent during the first year - almost half of these at the beginning of their studies. Altogether, ten percent had already completed five or more years of study before going abroad on an ERASMUS grant.

Table 3.5
Study Period in Major Field of Study Completed Prior to Study Period Abroad, by Country of Home University (percentage)

	\multicolumn{11}{c}{Country of home university}										Total
	B	D	DK	E	F	GR	I	IRL	NL	P	UK	
Beginner	1	10	0	5	5	3	2	0	2	10	5	5
< 1 year	0	6	2	4	4	0	13	7	2	0	10	6
1 - 1.9 years	2	13	0	2	12	3	5	29	7	0	25	12
2 - 2.9 years	11	30	39	9	43	11	14	32	18	20	54	32
3 - 3.9 years	16	23	20	19	21	22	27	15	21	10	4	18
4 - 4.9 years	56	11	27	38	10	30	21	12	27	20	1	16
5 - 5.9 years	9	5	9	16	4	16	11	2	15	30	0	7
6 - 6.9 years	2	1	2	5	1	3	5	2	6	0	0	2
7 and more years	0	0	0	2	1	14	3	0	1	10	0	1
Total	100	100	100	100	100	100	100	100	100	100	100	100
(n)	(211)	(775)	(44)	(304)	(665)	(37)	(281)	(41)	(154)	(10)	(630)	(3152)

Question 2.1/2.2: How long was the period of study you had completed in your major field of study prior to your ERASMUS supported period abroad (in years and months)?

The average length of study prior to the study period abroad was 2.7 years. This varied according to home country, from 1.8 years in the case of the United Kingdom to 4.4 years in the case of Greece. To summarize:

- only very few British students had completed more than two years of study when they went abroad due to the relatively short study periods in England and Wales to attain the first degree. Also, Irish students (2.4 years on average) went abroad after relatively short periods of prior study
- most French and German students went abroad during their third or fourth year of study (after 2.4 years on average)
- the prior length of study is widely spread in the case of Italian (mean of 3.3), Danish (3.4) and Dutch (3.7) students
- the majority of Greek (mean of 4.4), Portuguese, Belgian (3.8 each) and Spanish students (3.6) completed four or more years of study before they went abroad.

In general, the stage at which students have to go abroad (in accordance with arrangements made by the partner institutions as to when the students themselves choose to go, the arrangements between the institutions allow various stages), will be influenced by the special emphases of the individual programmes or individual students. In addition, the duration of degree programmes plays a role, as is most obvious in the case of the United Kingdom. Further, departments planning a study abroad period for large numbers of students, in some cases even mandatory study periods abroad for all students, usually provided for a study period as a rule not later than in the third year. This explains why the majority of German and French students went abroad at an earlier stage of their study than Portuguese, Greek, Spanish and Belgian students; many students of the latter countries go abroad after completion of a first degree.

Finally, there were different patterns according to the field of study. Students in business studies went abroad earliest in their course of study: more than a third each during the third year or earlier, whereas study periods at relatively late stages were most often reported by students in agriculture, architecture, fine arts, geography and geology, law, and medical sciences. The early stage of study abroad in the case of business studies, however, does not merely reflect characteristics of the discipline i.e. a belief that an experience abroad can be worthwhile at a relatively early stage of knowledge acquisition, but also organizational patterns. The quota of students going abroad in the framework of highly organized and mandatory arrangements is highest in business studies.

3.4   Duration and Activities Abroad

On average, students surveyed spent 7.1 months abroad in the
framework of the ERASMUS grant scheme. As Table 3.6 shows, 91
percent spent between 3 and 12 months abroad, i.e. a period considered
to be the rule in 1988/89. Three percent spent less than two months (as
reported in Chapter 2, persons studying abroad for less than one month
were excluded on the assumption that they received support in the
framework of intensive programmes rather than regular ERASMUS
student fellowships), while six percent reported a stay abroad supported
by ERASMUS for more than one year. In some of these cases, students
reported a longer period, although the support as such was not linked to
more than 12 months; in other cases, students from those programmes
named a longer period in which more than one study period abroad was
required and renewed application was made for support of the same
students.

Table 3.6
**Duration of Period Abroad Supported by ERASMUS, by Country of Home
University** (percentage)

	Country of home university											Total
	B	D	DK	E	F	GR	I	IRL	NL	P	UK	
1-2 months	1	3	0	4	1	0	2	5	11	0	4	3
3 months	37	14	14	21	21	44	28	31	21	0	23	21
4-6 months	54	41	65	37	23	11	50	44	61	20	24	36
7-12 months	8	36	21	35	45	44	18	21	7	80	41	34
More than 12 months	0	7	0	4	10	0	1	0	0	0	8	6
Total	100	100	100	100	100	100	100	100	100	100	100	100
(n)	(212)	(797)	(43)	(311)	(667)	(36)	(284)	(39)	(156)	(10)	(632)	(3187)

Question 2.4: Please state the duration of the ERASMUS supported period abroad (including work
placement and holiday periods).

On average, Dutch (4.3 months) and Belgian students (4.4 months)
spent the shortest periods abroad. Duration above mean was reported
by French (8.5 months), Portuguese (8.1 months), British (7.9 months)

and German students (7.6 months). In most cases the high proportion of relatively long (9.2 months) study periods abroad by business studies students accounts for the difference.

Besides business studies a duration longer than the mean was reported by engineering students (7.5 months), and an average duration by natural science students (7.1 months). Students enrolled in languages (6.3 months), mathematics (6.1 months) and law (5.9 months) were abroad for about half a year on average. On the other hand, stays abroad of at most 3 months dominated in agriculture, architecture, fine arts, and communication sciences.

About 65 percent of the ERASMUS students were solely engaged in full-time study during the period abroad, a further 11 percent in part-time study, while 22 percent participated in work placement in the host country - 18 percent in addition to a study and four percent solely in that activity. A further two percent mentioned other study-related activities, such as work on theses. As Table 3.7 shows, work placements were most common among students in medical fields (48 %), business studies, natural sciences (34 % each), engineering and agriculture (27 % each).

The work placement periods lasted 4.5 months on average. 52 percent of those who participated reported work placement periods of 4-6 months, 41 percent shorter ones, while seven percent experienced even longer work placement periods in the host country. Among the five disciplines in which work placement was relatively often provided, the average duration of work placement periods varied from 5.1 months in business studies to 3.9 months in agriculture.

Table 3.7
Major Activities During the Study Period Abroad, by Field of Study (percentage)

	I	II	III	IV	V	VI	VII	VIII	IX	X	XI	XII	XIII	XIV	XV	XVI	Total
Full-time study	53	67	68	60	72	63	57	67	75	74	55	48	54	68	40	56	65
Part-time study	10	18	12	5	13	4	19	15	17	16	17	2	5	18	33	12	11
Work placement	17	4	10	1	3	12	0	6	0	0	14	28	14	5	0	6	4
Full-time study/ part-time study	0	0	0	0	0	0	0	1	0	0	0	0	0	0	0	1	0
Full-time study/ work placement	10	1	4	29	3	10	5	5	4	6	4	11	15	4	0	14	14
Part-time study/ work placement	0	5	4	3	5	5	14	4	2	2	1	9	5	4	13	8	4
Full-/part-time study/work placement	0	0	0	1	0	0	0	0	0	0	0	0	0	0	0	0	0
Other	10	6	2	0	5	5	5	2	1	2	8	0	7	1	13	3	2
Total	100	100	100	100	100	100	100	100	100	100	100	100	100	100	100	100	100
(n)	(30)	(102)	(50)	(1039)	(39)	(310)	(21)	(113)	(570)	(337)	(76)	(46)	(136)	(125)	(15)	(155)	(3164)

I = Agricultural sciences	IX = Languages, philological sciences
II = Architecture, urban and regional planning	X = Law
III = Art and design	XI = Mathematics, informatics
IV = Business studies, management sciences	XII = Medical sciences
V = Education, teacher training	XIII = Natural sciences
VI = Engineering, technology	XIV = Social Sciences
VII = Geography, geology	XV = Communication and information sciences
VIII = Humanities	XVI = Other areas of study

Question 2.6: What were your major activities during the study period abroad (multiple reply possible)?

3.5   Select Biographical Information

54 percent of the respondents were female. As women comprise hardly
more than 45 percent of all students at institutions of higher education
in the European Community, the ERASMUS programme clearly has on
average higher participation rates of female than of male students.

The percentage of women among all ERASMUS students from
various countries ranged from 66 percent in the United Kingdom and 57
percent in France to 20 percent in Portugal and 23 percent in Denmark.
As one would expect, however, the differences according to home
country strongly reflected the composition according to field of study.
Women were most often represented in foreign language fields (83 %),
as Chart 3.1 shows, followed by fine arts, education, humanities and
communication sciences. They were least represented in engineering
(16 %), mathematics, and geography and geology.

Chart 3.1
Gender of the ERASMUS Students, by Field of Study (percentage)

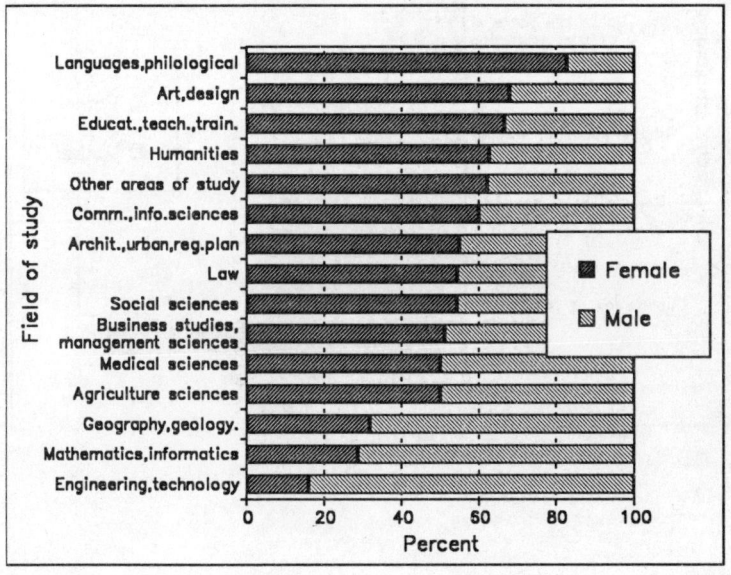

About 35 percent of the surveyed ERASMUS students reported that their father had completed a degree at an institution of higher education, while only 17 percent stated that their mothers were university trained. This finding was not specific to the parents of ERASMUS students, but reflects different educational opportunities between men and women in the parents' generation. The proportion of ERASMUS students whose parents merely had compulsory education (and possible subsequently vocational training) was remarkably high, as Chart 3.2 shows. It suggests that the ERASMUS programme does not merely serve the students from high socio-ecomomic backgrounds.

Chart 3.2
Fathers' and Mothers' Educational Attainment (total, percentage)

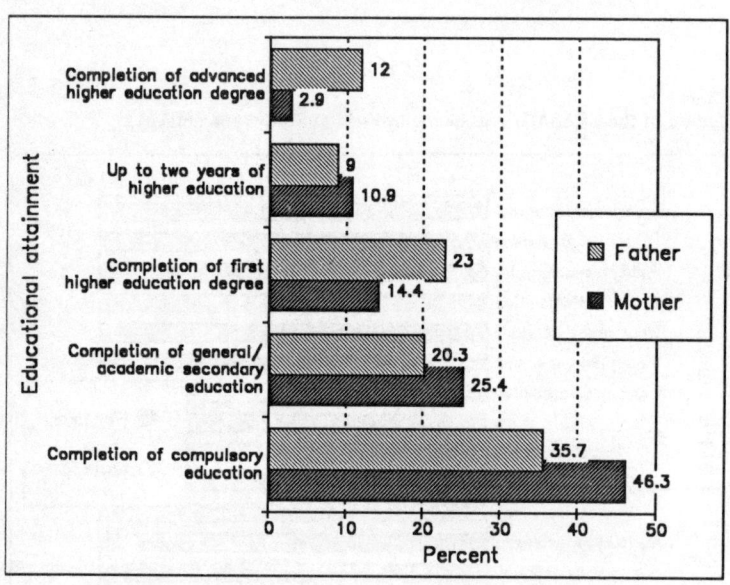

Around 14 percent of students reported that both parents were graduates from institutions of higher education, and in a further 23 percent of the cases, only the fathers or, in a few exceptional cases (3 %) mothers were graduates. The percentage of students with higher education-trained parents (either one or both of them) varied sub-stantially according to home country, as Table 3.8 shows. It was by far the highest in Greece (54 %) and Belgium (51 %), between 30 and 40 percent in the majority of EC Member States, and lowest in the Netherlands and Denmark (21 % each).

Table 3.8
Parents Higher Education Attainment, by Country of Home University
(percentage)

| | Country of home university | | | | | | | | | | | Total |
	B	D	DK	E	F	GR	I	IRL	NL	P	UK	
Both	15	10	5	15	18	30	17	15	1	20	17	14
Father	35	20	16	22	20	24	18	12	19	20	18	20
Mother	1	2	0	4	2	0	5	0	1	0	5	3
None	48	68	79	60	60	46	60	73	79	60	60	62
Total	100	100	100	100	100	100	100	100	100	100	100	100
(n)	(212)	(791)	(43)	(310)	(650)	(37)	(280)	(41)	(147)	(10)	(621)	(3142)

Question 1.4: What is the highest level of education attained by your father and mother?

ERASMUS students were also asked whether they had been engaged in any other activities besides a general educational career pattern for at least six consecutive months. As Table 3.9 shows, altogether 23 percent had been engaged in one or several of those activities:
- ten percent were employed for some period (most often Danish, Irish, British and German respondents)
- seven percent spent some period in military service, etc. (notably German and Danish students)
- six percent participated in vocational training (again mostly Danish and German students)

- five percent reported extended travel (most often Danish students, and also above mean British and German students, with France and the United Kingdom the most frequent sites of such travels)
- one percent each reported extended periods of unemployment and care of household and children, while four percent mentioned other activities.

As one might expect, a larger proportion of male students (29 %) had been engaged in those activities than female students (18 %). About 16 percent of men (no women) served in the military etc., seven percent (as compared with 5 % of the women) took vocational training, and 11 percent (as compared to 9 %) were employed. Two percent of women (no men) reported extended periods caring for households and children.

Table 3.9
Previous Activities Outside Educational Career Pattern, by Country of Home University (percentage)

				Country of home university								Total
	B	D	DK	E	F	GR	I	IRL	NL	P	UK	
Vocational training	1	17	14	3	0	3	2	5	1	0	3	6
Employment	0	14	32	7	4	8	4	20	3	0	18	10
Unemployment	0	1	5	1	0	0	0	2	0	0	4	1
Military service, etc.	0	23	11	3	3	0	4	2	0	0	0	7
Care of household/children	0	0	0	0	0	0	1	0	3	0	3	1
Travel	2	7	23	4	3	0	2	2	2	0	9	5
Other	3	7	7	4	3	0	5	2	9	0	2	4
Not ticked	95	55	55	83	89	89	87	73	86	100	75	77
Total	102	124	145	104	103	100	105	107	103	100	114	111
(n)	(216)	(801)	(44)	(312)	(673)	(37)	(285)	(41)	(156)	(10)	(637)	(3212)

Question 1.5: Before you studied abroad within ERASMUS, had you spent any period of at least 6 consecutive months doing something which was not part of the general educational career pattern you are following?

The average duration of those activities by the persons engaged was 32 months for care of household and children, 25 months for vocational training, 24 months for employment, 16 months for military service etc., 11 months for employment and, finally, ten months for travel. On average, of all ERASMUS students, almost half a year (exactly 5.2 months) was spent on activities other than their regular educational courses.

Around 80 percent of ERASMUS students reported that they had spent some period abroad prior to the ERASMUS-supported period since they were 15 years old; 48 percent had spent a previous period in the host country of the ERASMUS sojourn. The average total duration of stays abroad was 6.1 months (for all respondents), with 1.9 months spent in the subsequent host country. Prior stays abroad abroad varied to some extent by home country. Notably, students from various southern European countries had less experience of staying in foreign countries, as Chart 3.3 indicates.

Chart 3.3
Months Spent Abroad since the Age of 15, by Country of Home University (mean)

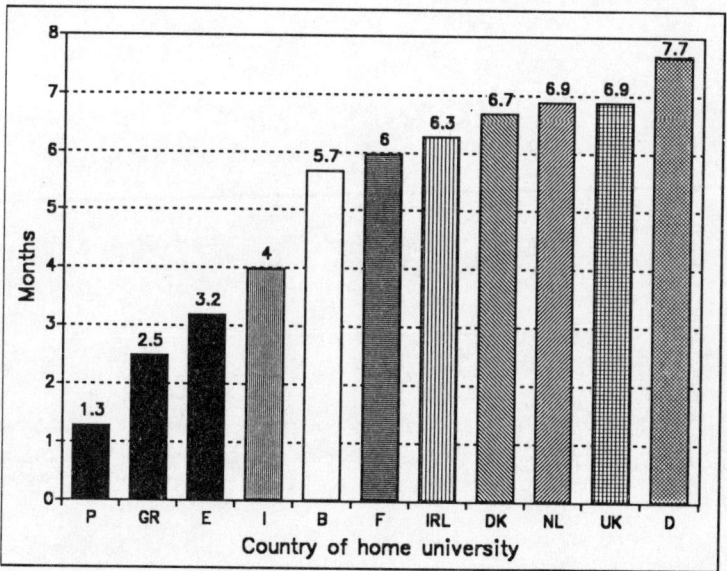

Ten percent of the students lived with a partner immediately before the ERASMUS-supported period abroad, and one percent had children at that time. While six percent of those going abroad during their first year of study had lived with a partner prior to the study abroad period, the respective ratio was 18 percent among students who already had completed at least six years of study prior to the ERASMUS-supported period abroad.

Almost half left their partner behind in the home country and more than half left their children in the home country while studying abroad. Altogether, these data suggest that students who live with a partner, as well as students who have children, rarely opt for a (ERASMUS-supported) study period abroad.

Chapter 4

Academic and Administrative Support

4.1 Ways and Areas of Preparation

As a rule, students need to anticipate life and study abroad and prepare themselves in various ways prior to the study abroad period; it is recognized that preparation helps reduce feelings of uncertainty and ensures that the knowledge necessary to ease integration and to cope with the academic requirements during the study period abroad is acquired. In the framework of the Inter-University Cooperation Programmes under the ERASMUS programme, most home universities offer preparatory courses, arrange preparatory meetings and possibly provide written material for the students' preparation.

The survey shows that:

- 67 percent of the ERASMUS students prepared themselves through self-study
- 58 percent made use of written material provided
- 51 percent attended mandatory courses of preparation for the study period abroad
- 44 percent took part in preparatory meetings
- 33 percent attended optional preparatory courses.

In looking at the proportions of students having made use of the most organized preparatory provisions, we note that:

- 51 percent of the ERASMUS students participated in mandatory preparatory courses
- 16 percent participated at least in optional preparatory courses giving an overall 66 percent participation in preparatory courses

- 13 percent at least attended preparatory meetings. Thus, altogether 79 percent participated in preparatory meetings and courses
- a further 16 percent prepared themselves for the study period abroad without attending meetings and courses, although possibly with the help of written material provided
- five percent stated that they went abroad without any specific preparation for the study period in the host country.

The data available do not allow us to examine how many students actually could have made use of courses or meetings before the study abroad period. Certainly, some students did not prepare themselves, although offers were made by their institution, and some prepared themselves through self-study, possibly with the help of written material provided, although they could have attended courses or meetings as well.

Participation in preparatory courses or meetings seemed to be an exception in the case of Portuguese students (only one out of eight students who responded); they were also attended by less than two-thirds of Belgian (57 %), Irish (62 %) and Dutch students (63 %). We assume that few preparatory courses were offered in those countries. Highest participation rates in preparatory courses and meetings were reported by British (87 %) Danish and French students (84 % each).

The longer the study period in the host country, the more likely students were to attend preparatory courses. As Chart 4.1 shows, less than half of the students going abroad for at most two months took preparatory courses (not including occasional meetings) in comparison with more than three quarters of those going abroad for more than half a year.

More than two thirds of participants in preparatory courses reported that at least some of those courses were part of the regular course programme. This was most often reported by French (83 %) and British students (79 %). Only 15 percent of Greek students had preparatory courses recognized as part of their regular course programme. Also, the integration of preparatory courses into the regular course programme was less often reported by Spanish (53 %) and Irish students (54 %) than by students from the remaining countries.

Chart 4.1
Participation of ERASMUS Students in Organized Preparation, by Duration of the Study Period Abroad (percentage)

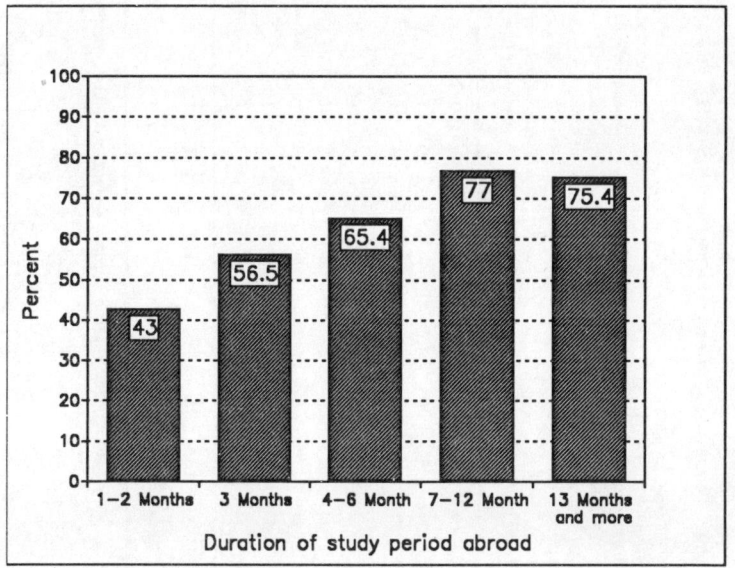

Students were asked to specify their ways of preparation in terms of four different topics:
- 78 percent prepared themselves through learning a foreign language
- 67 percent regarding practical matters of living in the host country and studying at the host university
- 67 percent as regards culture and society of the host country
- 61 percent reported academic preparation.

Academic and foreign-language preparation was done in most cases with the help of courses provided. In contrast, preparation regarding the host country's culture and society or regarding practical matters were mostly based on meetings, the provisions of written material, or on students' own initiatives in collecting information.

As Table 4.1 shows, participation in academic preparation did not differ much according to fields of study. Only in agriculture (30 %) and arts and design (36 %), did very few students report that they prepared

Table 4.1
Ways of Academic Preparation, by Field of Study (percentage)

	Major field during study period abroad																Total
	I	II	III	IV	V	VI	VII	VIII	IX	X	XI	XII	XIII	XIV	XV	XVI	
Written material	3	25	13	21	33	20	24	18	25	20	16	29	23	27	47	18	22
Meetings	7	20	11	14	23	11	14	15	15	17	8	9	13	19	27	16	15
Courses: mandatory	10	14	9	36	33	25	38	22	42	21	25	27	22	15	20	37	30
Courses: optional	3	6	2	9	11	11	14	16	13	21	13	18	7	13	0	11	12
Self-study	20	32	13	18	38	24	19	40	27	27	29	47	33	22	20	20	24
Not ticked	70	39	64	41	26	43	33	35	32	36	42	31	38	41	47	43	39
Total	113	135	111	139	187	133	143	145	153	141	133	160	135	138	160	145	142
(n)	(30)	(101)	(47)	(1018)	(39)	(293)	(21)	(110)	(554)	(323)	(76)	(45)	(133)	(120)	(15)	(148)	(3073)

I	=	Agricultural sciences	
II	=	Architecture, urban and regional planning	
III	=	Art and design	
IV	=	Business studies, management sciences	
V	=	Education, teacher training	
VI	=	Engineering, technology	
VII	=	Geography, geology	
VIII	=	Humanities	

IX	=	Languages, philological sciences
X	=	Law
XI	=	Mathematics, informatics
XII	=	Medical sciences
XIII	=	Natural sciences
XIV	=	Social Sciences
XV	=	Communication and information sciences
XVI	=	Other areas of study

Question 3.1: How did you prepare yourself prior to your stay abroad for the study period abroad? Which courses did you attend?

themselves academically. On the other hand, students of education and teacher training most often reported academic preparation (74 %) although surprisingly the participation in academic preparation did not vary according to the duration of the study period abroad (see Chart 4.2).

Students going to the Netherlands, Denmark, Belgium, Greece, and Ireland were most likely to report that there was no preparatory foreign language tuition. These were also the host countries for which the home universities least often prescribed participation in mandatory foreign language courses, as Table 4.2 shows. Obviously, it was not a widespread knowledge of the host country languages which accounted for this pattern. Rather, in most of these host countries for which foreign language preparation was least common, some universities had opted to offer at least part of the courses for ERASMUS students in languages different from the host country language.

Chart 4.2
Participation in (Mandatory and/or Optional) Courses Regarding Academic Matters, Foreign Language, Host Country Culture and Society and Practical Matters of Living and Studying Abroad, by Duration of the Study Period Abroad (percentage)

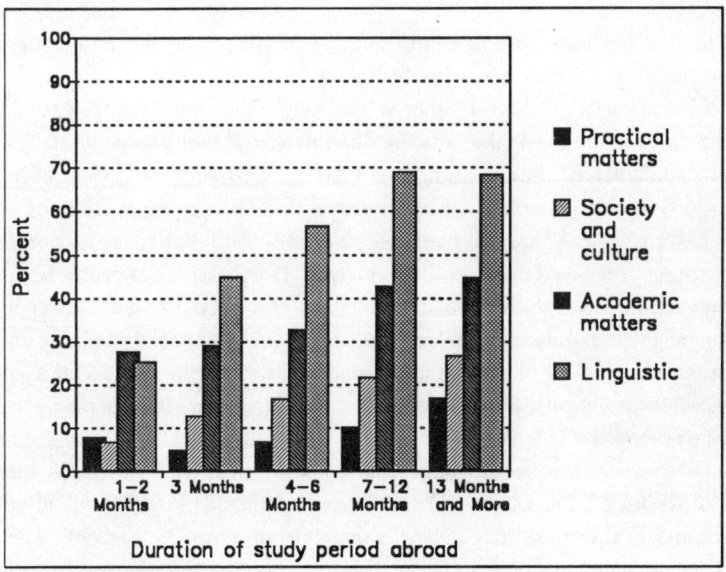

Table 4.2
Ways of Linguistic Preparation, by Host Country (percentage)

	B	D	DK	E	F	GR	I	IRL	NL	P	UK	Total
						Host country						Total
Written material	16	23	10	20	20	22	26	8	11	22	15	18
Meetings	6	8	7	8	7	5	6	3	3	5	4	6
Courses: mandatory	22	44	7	45	47	27	45	24	19	37	43	41
Courses: optional	21	26	10	32	28	30	20	27	13	32	24	25
Self-study	34	48	40	47	44	42	52	43	35	41	41	44
Not ticked	40	20	43	16	17	35	14	35	50	10	21	22
Total	139	168	117	168	163	163	163	139	130	146	148	156
(n)	(89)	(361)	(30)	(305)	(804)	(40)	(206)	(105)	(171)	(41)	(923)	(3075)

Question 3.1: How did you prepare yourself prior to your stay abroad for the study period abroad? Which courses did you attend?

Foreign language preparation, notably participation in mandatory preparatory courses, was closely linked to the duration of the study period abroad, as Chart 4.2 shows. The longer the study period abroad, the more likely it was that students had prepared themselves by means of mandatory or optional language courses. Certainly, one could have argued that students needed less in terms of language preparation for a relatively long phase abroad, because they had better chances of learning the language while abroad. Obviously, however, both universities and students had recognized the need for good foreign language preparation for a relatively long period abroad, because in those cases lack of understanding would be most detrimental, as far as a possible prolongation of the overall duration of the study period was concerned.

Mandatory foreign language courses were most often provided for British (63 %), French (51 %) and German students (36 %). In all other countries, the respective quota ranged from 0 to 29 percent. The frequent provision of mandatory language courses notably for British and French students might to some extent reflect limits in the previous foreign language competencies of students from these countries. In addition, one should bear in mind that a large proportion of British, French and German ERASMUS students participated in course programmes with mandatory study abroad components which are also more likely to incorporate elements of mandatory preparation.

Support for preparation regarding practical matters of living and studying abroad varied most strongly by home country. German, British and Danish students made more use of written materials or more frequently attended preparatory meetings than ERASMUS students from the other EC Member States. As Table 4.3 shows, a high proportion of British students attended preparatory courses for these purposes (55 % compared with 32 % of all ERASMUS students), while German students most frequently made use of written materials (64 % compared with 38 % of all ERASMUS students).

Table 4.3
Ways of Preparation: Practical Matters of Living and Studying in Host Country, by Country of Home University (percentage)

	Country of home university											Total
	B	D	DK	E	F	GR	I	IRL	NL	P	UK	
Written material	26	64	51	15	19	19	27	27	39	13	44	38
Meetings	27	35	54	30	19	17	17	24	28	0	55	32
Courses: mandatory	1	5	11	5	8	3	4	0	0	0	8	6
Courses: optional	1	8	5	5	3	0	3	0	1	0	3	4
Self-study	22	38	41	33	23	36	28	38	25	25	24	29
Not ticked	39	14	22	41	52	50	43	35	30	75	24	33
Total	117	164	184	128	124	125	121	124	123	113	159	142
(n)	(193)	(789)	(37)	(291)	(643)	(36)	(282)	(37)	(147)	(8)	(612)	(3075)

Question 3.1: How did you prepare yourself prior to your stay abroad for the study period abroad? Which courses did you attend?

Table 4.4
Ways of Preparation: Society and Culture of Host Country, by Field of Study (percentage)

	Major field during study period abroad																Total
	I	II	III	IV	V	VI	VII	VIII	IX	X	XI	XII	XIII	XIV	XV	XVI	
Written material	13	28	38	31	26	24	19	19	27	23	26	24	23	24	7	23	27
Meetings	7	5	11	12	18	10	0	15	12	7	7	0	7	9	13	14	11
Courses: mandatory	0	3	2	16	21	4	5	14	30	5	8	2	11	3	0	12	14
Courses: optional	0	2	2	4	28	5	5	4	9	7	4	7	7	7	5	5	6
Self-study	33	55	51	39	49	42	48	51	40	45	34	38	38	50	40	30	41
Not ticked	50	29	28	32	21	38	38	27	28	40	43	40	42	33	53	44	34
Total	103	122	132	135	162	123	114	130	147	125	122	111	127	127	113	128	133
(n)	(30)	(101)	(47)	(1018)	(39)	(293)	(21)	(110)	(554)	(323)	(76)	(45)	(133)	(120)	(15)	(148)	(3073)

I = Agricultural sciences
II = Architecture, urban and regional planning
III = Art and design
IV = Business studies, management sciences
V = Education, teacher training
VI = Engineering, technology
VII = Geography, geology
VIII = Humanities

IX = Languages, philological sciences
X = Law
XI = Mathematics, informatics
XII = Medical sciences
XIII = Natural sciences
XIV = Social Sciences
XV = Communication and information sciences
XVI = Other areas of study

Question 3.1: How did you prepare yourself prior to your stay abroad for the study period abroad? Which courses did you attend?

Preparatory courses or meetings giving information about the culture and society of the host country were most often attended by students from education and teacher training, languages and philologies as well and from other humanities, as Table 4.4 shows. Also, the frequent use of printed materials by art and design students indicated the impact of the field of study on the value which is placed on preparation regarding the host culture and society. One should add, however, that a relatively high proportion of British students attended mandatory courses (25 % compared with 13 % of all ERASMUS students) or occasional meetings (18 % compared with 10 %) to prepare themselves regarding the host country culture and society. This seemed to be due to the British tradition of higher education emphasizing a broad concept of socialisation of personality beyond the teaching and learning of disciplinary knowledge. Finally, preparation both for host country culture and society as well as for practical matters was somewhat less likely if the duration of study period abroad was relatively short (see Chart 4.2).

4.2 Assessment of Preparatory Provisions

Students rated the foreign language provisions at their home university more positively than other preparatory provisions. They rated the foreign language provisions on average 2.6 on a scale from 1 = "very good" to 5 = "very poor" compared with 2.8 for academic preparation, 3.0 for preparation for host country culture and society, and 3.2 for preparation for practical matters. The findings, first, suggest that the ratings were better the more highly organized the preparatory provisions. Second, the mean scores were so close to the centre of the scale, that improvement of preparatory provisions was needed at many universities, according to the students' views.

The assessment of the preparatory provisions varied most strongly by the home country of the ERASMUS students. Irish and Spanish students rated the preparatory provisions most negatively (as Table 4.5 shows), while Belgian and Greek students assessed the preparatory provisions at their home institutions most favourably.

It should be noted that assessment of the preparatory provisions did not differ strongly according to the host country nor according to the duration of the study period abroad, suggesting that the criticism of the preparatory provisions was not much influenced by specific experiences abroad. We might add, finally, that students from a few fields of study rated the preparatory provisions most negatively: notably those from agriculture, from geology and geography, and those from the humanities.

Table 4.5
Assessment of Preparatory Provision, by Country of Home University (mean*)

	Country of home university											Total
	B	D	DK	E	F	GR	I	IRL	NL	P	UK	
Living/studying preparation	3.1	3.2	2.8	3.6	3.2	3.0	2.9	3.8	3.3	3.0	3.2	3.2
Culture preparation	2.6	3.1	2.3	3.5	2.8	2.7	2.7	3.8	2.9	2.0	2.9	3.0
Academic preparation	2.8	3.0	2.7	2.9	2.8	2.3	2.6	2.9	2.9	3.0	2.7	2.8
Linguistic preparation	2.4	2.6	2.5	3.0	2.4	2.5	2.6	3.2	2.8	3.0	2.5	2.6
Other preparation	2.7	3.0	3.3	3.2	2.8	2.4	2.6	3.5	2.8	3.0	2.9	2.9

Question 3.2: How do you assess the preparatory provision?

* On a scale from 1 = "very good" to 5 = "very poor"

4.3   Assistance and Advice Provided by the Host University

Assistance, guidance and advice by the host university might be even more important for the success of the study period in another country than the preparation prior to that period. Students were asked to state both the extent to which they were provided assistance and advice abroad, and the degree of satisfaction they felt with that assistance, guidance and advice.

ERASMUS students were provided with a list of 13 categories, which refer - like the questions about preparation - to academic issues, foreign language, host culture and society, as well as practical matters abroad. In addition, students were asked about the advice and assistance provided by the host university regarding personal matters. While foreign language, academic and personal matters were referred to in an aggregate way, the questionnaire addressed specific aspects of assistance and advice regarding:

- living and studying abroad: orientation about the host university and the host country's higher education system, issues of registration, and course selection etc., accommodation, matters regarding students' financial support, work placement, and other practical matters (insurance, registration with civil authorities, etc); and
- culture and society of the host country: the host country in general, the local community, social contacts with host country nationals, and finally cultural, sports and recreational activities.

Altogether, very few ERASMUS students reported minimal assistance and advice by the host university: only two percent reported little assistance regarding the practical matters addressed in the questionnaire, eight percent regarding any aspects which referred to the host country culture and society, and 11 percent in academic matters. However, support and advice regarding language training as well as regarding personal matters were less often provided: 31 percent and 46 percent respectively stated that they had no assistance and guidance in those respects.

Turning to the individual aspects addressed in the questionnaire (see Table 4.6), we note that students reported that assistance and guidance were most common regarding:

- university registration, course selection, etc.
- academic matters.

Table 4.6
Assistance/Guidance/Advice Provided by Host University, by Host Country (percentage)

	Host country											Total
	B	D	DK	E	F	GR	I	IRL	NL	P	UK	
University registration etc. at host univ.												
Substantial	61	40	56	37	42	51	31	66	52	18	60	48
Modest	28	48	34	47	41	36	47	28	37	57	33	40
None	11	12	9	17	17	13	22	6	11	25	7	13
Living accommodation												
Substantial	61	61	71	17	49	51	51	55	55	31	61	52
Modest	27	24	23	35	31	23	28	36	32	38	28	30
None	12	15	6	48	20	26	21	9	14	31	10	18
Matters regarding students financial support												
Substantial	16	15	23	6	10	15	9	16	18	6	14	12
Modest	28	34	39	23	26	38	23	31	27	27	34	29
None	55	50	39	71	64	47	68	53	55	67	52	58
Other practical matters (e.g. insurance etc.)												
Substantial	26	24	50	10	14	15	20	21	27	3	25	20
Modest	31	44	30	31	37	38	41	45	29	26	39	37
None	43	32	20	59	49	47	39	35	44	71	36	43
(to be cont.)												

(Table 4.6 cont.)

	B	D	DK	E	F	GR	I	IRL	NL	P	UK	Total
					Host country							
Academic matters												
Substantial	51	36	65	31	34	49	31	49	44	23	55	42
Modest	36	50	35	58	52	49	56	39	47	51	40	48
None	13	14	0	11	14	2	13	12	9	26	6	11
Work placement matters (if applicable)												
Substantial	31	33	67	30	34	22	22	29	43	31	36	34
Modest	17	28	17	42	32	44	37	29	27	25	39	34
None	52	40	17	28	33	33	41	42	30	44	25	32
Orientation on the host country univ.												
Substantial	36	32	58	17	18	27	13	31	28	22	36	27
Modest	39	45	29	46	49	54	47	48	46	50	49	47
None	25	23	13	37	33	20	40	21	26	28	15	26
Language training												
Substantial	45	37	43	33	34	31	30	47	19	11	34	34
Modest	22	35	29	37	33	33	31	24	29	31	40	35
None	32	27	29	30	33	36	38	29	52	57	26	31
The host country in general												
Substantial	33	25	50	24	16	44	20	38	30	25	21	22
Modest	48	50	44	49	51	47	42	42	47	50	55	51
None	20	24	6	27	33	9	38	20	23	25	24	27

(to be cont.)

(Table 4.6 cont.)

| | Host country | | | | | | | | | | | Total |
	B	D	DK	E	F	GR	I	IRL	NL	P	UK	
The local community												
Substantial	24	22	38	26	15	33	19	30	25	27	20	21
Modest	46	40	31	44	42	45	34	48	44	35	49	44
None	30	38	31	30	42	21	47	22	31	38	31	35
Personal matters												
Substantial	30	20	40	16	10	17	15	26	19	15	23	18
Modest	34	31	30	33	31	43	27	44	35	32	46	36
None	35	49	30	51	58	40	59	29	46	53	31	46
Social contacts with host country nationals												
Substantial	31	30	37	32	20	38	24	42	32	24	22	26
Modest	45	36	33	37	46	33	28	36	43	30	44	41
None	24	34	30	31	34	29	48	22	25	46	34	33
Cultural, sports, recreational activities												
Substantial	43	40	27	27	32	35	16	66	32	24	62	42
Modest	33	38	43	41	45	37	32	23	44	22	31	37
None	24	22	30	32	23	28	52	11	23	54	7	21

Question 4.2: To what extent were you provided with assistance/guidance/advice by your host university? And to what extent were you satisfied with the assistance/guidance/advice provided?

Only 13 percent and 11 percent respectively reported no support at all. Assistance and guidance was also widespread regarding two further aspects, though 18 percent and 21 percent respectively did not experience any assistance and advice concerning:
- accommodation
- cultural, sports and recreational activities.

As regards some aspects, provisions varied substantially. Almost equal numbers mentioned substantial support on the one hand and no assistance and advice at all on the other regarding five aspects:
- language training
- orientation on the host university and the host country's higher education system
- the host country in general
- social contacts with host country nationals
- work placement matters (if applicable).

No assistance and guidance was most often stated as regards:
- matters regarding students' financial support (58 % reported no assistance and advice at all)
- personal matters (46 %)
- other practical matters, such as insurance and registration with civil authorities (43 %)
- the local community (35 % as compared with 21 % reporting substantial assistance and advice).

Assistance, guidance and support varied substantially by host country. If we calculate the mean percentages of ERASMUS students not receiving assistance and guidance regarding the 13 aspects surveyed, we note that:
- students who went to Denmark (20 %), the United Kingdom and Ireland (23 % each) were least often left without support
- students going to Greece (27 %), Belgium, the Federal Republic of Germany (29 % each), and the Netherlands (30 %) were not often without assistance and advice
- students going to France (35 %) and Spain (36 %) reported more often that they did not experience assistance and advice
- no advice on many aspects was most common in Italy (40 %) and Portugal (44 %).

In the case of the four countries offering least assistance and guidance for the ERASMUS students they hosted, different patterns emerged:
- French universities offered somewhat less than average assistance and advice regarding most aspects without any aspect appearing considerably below average
- Spanish universities provided assistance and guidance far below average in various practical matters of living and studying abroad, notably regarding accommodation, but also in matters regarding students' financial support, and other practical matters. In addition, little orientation was provided regarding the host country
- Italian universities provided little assistance regarding all aspects of host country culture and society referred to in the questionnaire
- Portuguese universities provided little assistance and guidance for the incoming ERASMUS students in various areas, including most practical matters, some aspects of host country culture and society as well as academic matters.

Programmes which provided for a short stay of at most two months abroad, showed patterns of assistance and guidance which clearly differed from that provided for stays of three and more months (see Table 4.7). In the case of such short stays, assistance was usually provided on accommodation and issues of students' financial support as well as orientation about the host country, the community and social contacts to host country nationals. Host institutions wanted to make sure that students staying such a short time abroad had no administrative burdens and that students got to know the host culture and society without needing much initiative of their own. On the other hand, much less assistance in learning the host country language was provided for students going abroad for at most two months than those staying a longer period abroad.

Students from business fields and teacher training were more often given assistance and advice than students from other fields, notably as regards foreign language. Students from medical fields and those from communication and information sciences experienced least assistance and advice.

Table 4.7
Assistance/Guidance/Advice Provided by Host University, by Duration of Study Period Abroad (percentage)

	Duration of Study Abroad					
	1-2 months	3 months	4-6 months	7-12 months	13 and more months	Total
University registration etc. at host univ.						
Substantial	51	50	48	47	44	48
Modest	33	39	39	40	44	39
None	16	11	13	13	12	13
Living accommodation						
Substantial	62	55	50	53	41	52
Modest	27	28	30	29	37	30
None	11	18	20	18	22	18
Matters regarding students financial support						
Substantial	44	14	11	12	9	12
Modest	22	31	27	32	28	29
None	34	55	62	57	63	58
Other practical matters (e.g. insurance etc.)						
Substantial	25	22	20	21	9	20
Modest	34	32	37	39	52	37
None	42	46	43	40	39	43
Academic matters						
Substantial	56	44	41	42	34	42
Modest	30	47	48	48	59	48
None	14	9	12	11	7	11
Work placement matters (if applicable)						
Substantial	34	36	30	33	41	34
Modest	29	33	36	32	41	34
None	37	31	35	34	18	32
Orientation on the host country univ.						
Substantial	31	33	24	26	21	27
Modest	47	46	47	49	50	47
None	21	21	29	26	29	26

(To be cont.)

(Table 4.7 cont.)	Duration of Study Abroad					
	1-2 months	3 months	4-6 months	7-12 months	13 and more	Total
Language training						
Substantial	21	31	36	33	39	34
Modest	22	35	34	36	40	35
None	57	35	30	31	21	31
The host country in general						
Substantial	34	29	23	18	13	22
Modest	54	50	50	49	57	51
None	13	20	27	33	31	27
The local community						
Substantial	35	28	20	17	13	21
Modest	48	43	46	42	41	44
None	17	28	34	41	47	35
Personal matters						
Substantial	24	24	18	16	10	18
Modest	36	34	37	38	33	36
None	41	42	46	46	57	46
Social contacts with host country nationals						
Substantial	44	32	27	21	19	26
Modest	37	39	42	43	33	41
None	19	29	31	36	48	33
Cultural, sports, recreational activities						
Substantial	46	37	42	45	36	42
Modest	27	41	35	37	44	37
None	27	22	23	18	21	21

Question 4.2: To what extent were you provided with assistance/guidance/advice by your host university? And to what extent were you satisfied with the assistance/guidance/advice provided?

4.4　Satisfaction with Assistance and Advice Abroad

· Asked about the degree of satisfaction with the assistance provided by the host universities, ERASMUS students rated, on a scale from 1 = "very high" to 5 = "very low", assistance regarding:

- academic matters 2.5
- language training matters 2.7
- various aspects regarding host country culture and society 2.7
- various aspects regarding practical matters 2.8
- personal matters 2.8.

The ratings regarding the individual aspects are documented in Table 4.8.

The assessment of assistance by the host university was somewhat more positive than the rating of the preparatory provisions by the home university. As regards academic, cultural and practical matters, ratings of the assistance abroad were about 0.3 more positive than ratings of the preparatory provisions at home. The comparison, however, might be undertaken only with some caution because of the different phrasing of the scale and the aspects to be rated.

The degree of satisfaction with the assistance and advice provided by the host university was highly correlated with the amount of the assistance and advice provided. The respective correlation coefficients ranged from 0.6 to 0.8, indicating that a high degree of assistance and advice by the host institution was highly appreciated as a rule. There are, however, some cases in which strong efforts to provide assistance and advice were not highly appreciated. The ratings provided do not allow us to name the reasons for dissatisfaction in those cases, that is whether lesser assistance was preferred or whether the efforts made were considered as inefficient, inappropriate, not leading to the intended results or, on the contrary, to the kind of support the students would like.

Given the high correlation, it is not surprising to find a similar ranking of host countries, if we calculate the satisfaction by incoming students with the assistance provided on average for all aspects. Assistance provided by Danish and Irish universities was most highly appreciated (2.3 each on average), while the extent of assistance provided by Portuguese and Italian universities (3.1 each) as well as by Spanish and French universities (3.0 each) was most often criticised.

It is also not surprising to find that students going abroad for at most two months were most satisfied with the assistance provided by the host institutions. We note, however, that students spending four months or more abroad were more critical about the assistance provided in getting

Table 4.8
Degree of Satisfaction with Assistance/Guidance/Advice Provided by the Host University, by Host Country (mean*)

	B	D	DK	E	F	GR	I	IRL	NL	P	UK	Total
					Host country							
University registration etc. at host univ.	2.3	2.5	1.9	2.8	2.8	2.3	3.1	2.1	2.4	3.0	2.1	2.5
Living accommodation	2.5	2.2	2.2	3.6	2.8	2.7	2.8	2.4	2.7	3.2	2.2	2.6
Matters regarding students financial support	3.1	3.1	2.8	3.7	3.5	3.0	3.5	2.8	3.1	3.6	3.1	3.3
Other practical matters (e.g. insurance etc.)	3.1	2.9	2.5	3.4	3.4	2.8	3.4	2.5	2.8	3.7	2.6	3.0
Academic matters	2.2	2.5	2.0	2.6	2.9	2.3	2.9	2.1	2.4	2.8	2.0	2.5
Work placement matters (if applicable)	2.8	2.8	2.3	3.0	3.0	3.1	3.4	2.4	2.4	2.9	2.7	2.9
Orientation on the host country univ.	2.5	2.7	2.0	3.2	3.2	2.8	3.5	2.5	2.8	3.0	2.5	2.8
Language training	2.5	2.5	2.6	2.7	2.8	3.2	3.1	2.1	3.2	3.1	2.6	2.7
The host country in general	2.5	2.6	1.9	2.8	3.0	2.4	2.9	2.2	2.5	2.6	2.6	2.7
The local community	2.7	2.8	2.3	2.7	3.2	2.7	3.0	2.4	2.7	2.7	2.7	2.8
Personal matters	2.6	2.8	2.3	3.0	3.2	2.6	3.2	2.4	2.7	2.9	2.4	2.8
Social contacts with host country nationals	2.7	2.7	2.4	2.6	3.0	2.7	3.0	2.3	2.7	2.9	2.7	2.8
Cultural, sports, recreational activities	2.5	2.3	2.6	2.9	2.7	2.7	3.3	1.7	2.5	2.7	1.8	2.4

Question 4.2: To what extent were you provided with assistance/ guidance/advice by your host university? And to what extent were you satisfied with the assistance/guidance/advice provided?

* On a scale from 1 = "very high" to 5 = "very low"

to know the host country culture and society than one might have
expected on the basis of statements regarding the amount of assistance
provided. Obviously, students staying longer than a few months abroad
expected better means of assistance in getting to know the host country
than actually offered.

There were notable differences in the responses of male and female
students on this topic, with female students less satisfied with almost all
aspects of assistance by the host university. The higher expectations on
the part of women on the role of the host university is underscored by
the fact that female ERASMUS students varied much less from male
students in their statements regarding the amount of assistance
provided.

Although ERASMUS students were more satisfied with the
assistance provided by the host institutions than with the preparatory
provisions at their home universities, improvement in assistance on part
of the host universities was suggested in many cases. Obviously, most
ERASMUS students would appreciate a broad range of assistance and
advice, including help to get to know the host country and its culture,
and regarding personal matters.

Chapter 5

Study and Experiences in the Host Country

5.1 Cultural and Social Activities in the Host Country

It is recognized that ERASMUS students at a host university can experience the culture and society of the host country in a variety of ways. Learning about and experiencing the host country culture and society is necessary in order to cope with life and study there, as well as to serve one's own social and cultural needs during the study period, and is in itself a valuable area of learning which enriches the knowledge and competences in the long run.

Asked about various experiences and activities aimed at getting to know the host country, ERASMUS students mentioned a receptive strategy most often. Three quarters mentioned that they often listened to or read news about the host country, 68 percent often had discussions and conversations with students of the host country, 61 percent had frequent contacts with the teaching staff of the host country, and 57 reported frequent discussions and conversations with other people of the host country. Two-thirds of the ERASMUS students frequently visited museums or attended concerts, theatre, cinema, etc., and 59 percent frequently had joint leisure activities with host country nationals. About half of the ERASMUS students frequently travelled in the host country.

The frequency of such experiences and activities could be influenced by patterns of behaviour common in one's home country, by the characteristics of the host country, by behavioural modes or areas of interest associated to fields of study and, last but not least, by the duration of the study period abroad. In referring to the home country of the ERASMUS student, we note, for example, that German students most often listened to or read news about the host country (86 %), whereas Italian and Dutch students emphasized this way of gathering information less frequently (63 and 64 % respectively). Frequent contact with the teaching staff was reported by about three quarters of students who spent a study period in the United Kingdom (76 %) and in Greece (72 %), but only by about half of the students who went to France (48 %), Italy (50 %), Portugal (54 %), and Germany (54 %). Students who spent a period of study in Spain, most frequently (71 % as compared to 54 % of all ERASMUS students) reported that they often visited museums or attended concerts, theatre, cinema, etc.

Various cultural activities, such as visiting museums, attending concerts etc. varied, as expected, according to field of study. Students in art and design (84 %), education (77 %) and humanities (72 %) stated that they undertook those cultural activities often, as opposed to students of geology and geography (32 %), mathematics and information science (47 %) and agriculture (48 %). Frequent travelling in the host country was reported by about two thirds of students in geology and geography as well as by students in art and design, compared with about half of all ERASMUS students on average.

Reports about the frequency of experiences and activities aimed at getting to know the host country and to communicate with persons of the host country varied most markedly according to the duration of the study period in the host country. The longer the ERASMUS students stayed in the host country, the higher was the proportion stating that they listened to or read news about the host country (ranging from 41 % of those staying at most two months abroad to 86 % of those staying more than one year abroad). Table 5.1 further shows that students who spent at most two months abroad obviously had much less chance of getting to know the host country and experience its culture other than contacts in the university environment and travel in the host country.

Contacts in the academic context seemed to change in opposite directions in the course of the stay abroad. The shorter the duration of the study period abroad, the higher the proportion of ERASMUS students who experienced frequent contacts with teaching staff of the host country. On the other hand, frequent discussions and conversations with students of the host country were more often reported the longer the period abroad lasted. Obviously, the teaching staff at the host institution got in touch with the incoming students regarding various academic, administrative, social and personal matters, but only some of those contacts were sustained, while fellow students at the host institution became a more important reference group over the months.

Table 5.1
Experiences and Activities Abroad, by Duration of Study Period Abroad
(percentage*)

	Duration of study abroad					Total
	1-2 months	3 months	4-6 months	7-12 months	More than 12 months	
Contact with teaching staff of host country	70	62	61	60	55	61
Discussions/conversations with students of host country	59	63	63	74	84	68
Discussions/conversations with other people of host country	39	57	58	56	69	57
Listening to/reading news about host country	41	63	77	80	85	74
Travelling in host country	57	54	52	54	58	54
Visiting museums, attending concerts, theatre, cinema etc.	59	63	61	67	66	64
Joint leisure activities with host country nationals	48	57	57	61	70	59

Question 4.1: Please state the frequency of the following experiences and activities during your study period abroad.

* Percent 1+2 on a scale from 1 = "very often" to 5 = "not at all"

5.2   Study at the Host Institution

ERASMUS students participated in an average of 17.2 hours of courses (including laboratory work etc.) at the host institutions.

The weekly course load abroad was on average 3.4 hours less (17 % ·less) than that taken at the home university (20.6 hours). Also, the

information provided about the degree of recognition of study achievements abroad upon return suggested that ERASMUS students while
abroad successfully completed about five sixths of the courses they
would typically complete at their home institution (see Chapter 8). As
Chart 5.1 shows, only Dutch and Portuguese students took more course
hours abroad than at home - students of those countries in which the
students surveyed took least course hours at home (11.8 and 15.1 hours).
Conversely, French students reduced their course hours abroad the
most: by 7.2 hours or 27 percent - students of the country in which students took the most course hours at home (25.6 hours).

Chart 5.1
**Weekly Course Hours at Home and Host University, by Country of Home
University** (mean)

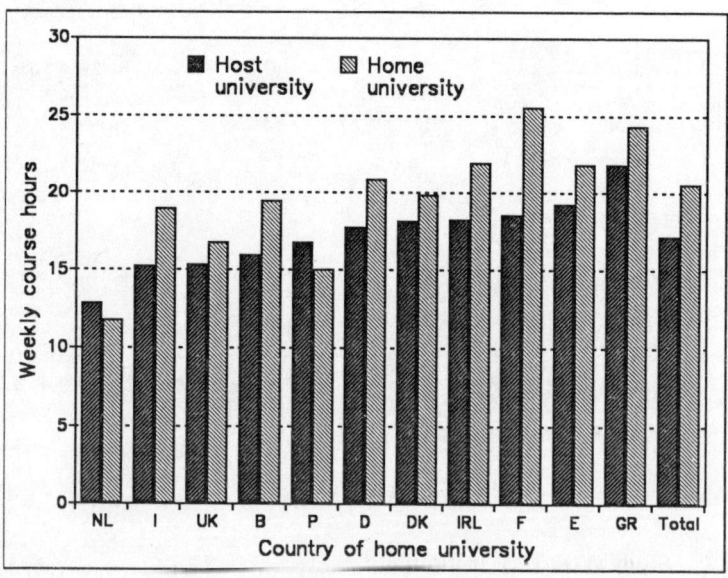

Students were also asked to estimate all weekly hours spent on various
types of study, including practical projects, foreign language learning,
independent study, work on theses, field trips etc. As Table 5.2 shows,

students reported 39 weekly hours spent on studies during regular working weeks at the host university.

Of this total, 17 hours were spent on attending courses. Nine hours were devoted to independent study, and about four hours each for practical projects and work on theses. Only 2.6 hours per week were spent on average for language training. The host country's educational styles had an impact on the distribution of study time abroad: most hours were spent on courses by students spending their study period abroad in France (18.1 hours), i.e. the country in which home students spent the most time on lectures. Conversely, students going to Portugal (12.3 hours), Greece (13.1 hours) and the Netherlands (13.7 hours) spent least time on lectures - those countries in which home students take the smallest number of courses (except Greece, which mostly offers special programmes for foreign students).

The type of study activities varied according to field of study notably regarding practical projects, laboratory work etc. This ranged from one weekly hour in law to 16 hours in agriculture and medical fields and 19 hours in natural sciences, as Table 5.2 shows. The average number of weekly hours spent for study was highest in fields of study which required substantial laboratory work.

Many students used the opportunity of studying at a university of an another EC Member State to participate in courses contrasting those offered at the home institution. As Table 5.3 shows, more than two-thirds of the ERASMUS students took courses involving content not available at the home university. About one half experienced new teaching methods, and a third utilized laboratories or other facilities not available or at a lesser quality at the home institution. In addition, about half of the students took courses to broaden their academic and cultural horizon which were not compulsory or directly linked to their area of specialization. 45 percent took courses in the host country language and 26 percent courses in other languages. About a fifth of the students reported that they developed a new area of specialization, and a tenth changed their earlier chosen specialization. Altogether, these findings were similar to those reported by students who participated in Joint Study Programmes in the mid-eighties.

Students going to Denmark (81 %) and Ireland (79 %) most frequently took courses involving content not available at their home university; the proportion was smallest among students going to

Table 5.2
Weekly Hours Spent on Study, by Field of Study (mean)

	Major field during study period abroad																Total
	I	II	III	IV	V	VI	VII	VIII	IX	X	XI	XII	XIII	XIV	XV	XVI	
Courses and course-related activities	9.4	9.9	8.8	20.5	15.8	15.4	11.9	13.9	15.2	19.3	14.6	12.3	11.8	13.2	9.9	14.3	16.7
Practical projects, laboratory work etc.	15.6	9.2	8.9	2.2	3.6	10.7	6.2	3.0	1.1	.8	7.9	16.3	19.2	1.7	3.7	4.7	4.3
Independent study	9.5	8.7	15.0	8.1	8.4	7.7	9.3	9.1	9.0	10.2	9.8	12.2	7.7	8.7	8.1	7.0	8.7
Work on thesis	8.5	3.9	1.4	3.2	5.1	5.5	2.6	5.9	3.7	3.5	3.1	5.9	3.8	5.8	13.5	3.6	3.9
Field trips, study-related excursions, observations	1.8	6.3	5.1	1.0	2.6	1.1	5.5	2.8	2.2	1.5	1.7	3.0	1.2	2.4	1.1	1.7	1.8
Language training	2.8	3.0	2.1	2.4	5.4	1.6	1.8	3.6	3.7	1.8	2.2	1.8	1.8	3.3	1.2	2.7	2.6
Other study activities	.3	2.2	3.1	.8	2.1	.7	1.7	1.8	.8	1.5	1.8	.6	.5	1.6	3.2	1.6	1.1
Total weekly hours	47.8	43.3	44.4	38.2	43.0	42.7	39.2	40.2	35.7	38.7	41.0	52.1	46.0	36.7	40.7	35.7	35.1

I	=	Agricultural sciences
II	=	Architecture, urban and regional planning
III	=	Art and design
IV	=	Business studies, management sciences
V	=	Education, teacher training
VI	=	Engineering, technology
VII	=	Geography, geology
VIII	=	Humanities
IX	=	Languages, philological sciences
X	=	Law
XI	=	Mathematics, informatics
XII	=	Medical sciences
XIII	=	Natural sciences
XIV	=	Social Sciences
XV	=	Communication and information sciences
XVI	=	Other areas of study

Question 4.3: How many hours per week did you spend on average on the following types of study? Please estimate for the academic study period only (i.e. excluding work placement and holiday periods).

Table 5.3
Type of Academic Enhancement During Study Period Abroad, by Host Country (percentage)

	Host country											Total
	B	D	DK	E	F	GR	I	IRL	NL	P	UK	
Take courses inv. content/topics not avail. at home univ.	75	69	81	63	69	54	67	79	72	52	67	68
Take courses inv. teaching meth. not practised at home u.	36	50	52	38	52	49	41	53	50	37	67	53
Utilize laboratories or other facilities (e.g. comp. data anal.)	32	33	23	15	22	36	14	25	35	4	48	31
Take courses to broaden acad. and cultural background	51	52	45	56	46	67	44	67	29	48	44	47
Develop a new area of specialization	31	17	35	14	24	21	21	14	34	22	19	21
Change an earlier chosen specialization	3	7	13	7	7	5	6	5	8	15	10	8
Take language courses in the host country language	36	50	52	50	48	46	44	54	18	26	44	45
Take language courses in other language	25	41	13	24	31	18	8	23	11	0	23	26
Total	290	320	313	267	300	295	247	322	259	204	323	299
(n)	(88)	(353)	(31)	(297)	(782)	(39)	(200)	(92)	(174)	(27)	(909)	(2992)

Question 4.5: During your study period abroad, did you ...? (multiple reply possible)

and Greece (54 %). Students going to the United Kingdom stated most often that they experienced teaching methods not common at home (67 %) and that they had access to facilities not available at home (48 %). Language courses in the host country language were least often taken by students going to the Netherlands (18 %), Portugal (26 %) and Belgium (36 %). In the case of the Netherlands and Belgium, this fitted in with the findings shown below, namely that relatively few ERASMUS students took courses there taught in the host country language or, at most, in combination with another language.

Table 5.4
Language of Instruction* During Study Period Abroad, by Host Country
(percentage)

	Host country											Total
	B	D	DK	E	F	GR	I	IRL	NL	P	UK	
Host	32	71	16	62	73	5	74	86	12	64	89	71
Home	29	1	26	0	7	10	4	2	41	6	1	6
Host+Home	8	4	0	6	4	0	6	1	7	6	2	4
Home+other	0	0	3	0	0	5	1	0	4	3	0	0
Host+other	10	19	16	22	11	5	12	7	5	6	6	11
Host+home +other	11	4	0	4	4	0	1	4	7	6	2	4
Other	10	1	39	6	0	75	2	0	25	11	0	4
Total	100	100	100	100	100	100	100	100	100	100	100	100
(n)	(90)	(356)	(31)	(305)	(818)	(40)	(206)	(103)	(169)	(36)	(944)	(3098)

Question 4.6: What was the language of instruction in the courses you took at the host university? If you were taught in more than one language, please state percentages.

* "Home" was coded if host country language and country of home university language were identical.

About 90 percent of the ERASMUS students took - at least in part - courses taught in the language of the host country, while 70 percent attended courses taught only in the host country language. As Table 5.4 shows, a mixture of languages prevailed if students were not taught solely in the host country language. Only six percent were solely taught in the home country language, and four percent solely in a third language (neither that of the host country nor that of the home country). Students from Belgium and Ireland were most often taught abroad in their home country language. This is not surprising because large proportions of ERASMUS students from these countries went to neighbouring countries with identical languages - in the former case to France and the Netherlands and in the latter case to the United Kingdom.

The host country language was least often (solely or partly) the language of instruction for students going to Greece (10 %), the Netherlands (31 %) and Denmark (32 %); in these cases English was frequently used as a language of instruction for incoming ERASMUS students. Among the relatively small host countries, the language of which is seldom taught in secondary schools in other EC Member States and is not widely used internationally, Portugal turned out to be an exception, for almost two-thirds of the ERASMUS students going to Portugal were taught in Portuguese.

The longer the study period in the host country, the more likely were courses to be given in the host country language. 20 percent of students going abroad for 1-2 months did not take any courses in the host country language, while the respective proportions were 16 percent for those going three months abroad, four percent for those going 4-6 months and three percent for those going 7-12 months. Conversely, the proportions of those solely taught in the host country language were 55, 61, 67 and 79 percent. It is obvious that short stays (at most three months) accounted for about half or even more of those students going to Greece, Portugal, Denmark and the Netherlands (see Chapter 3), i.e. those relatively small countries in the European Community whose languages are least common internationally.

5.3 Characteristics of Courses at Host Universities

To what extent do teaching and learning environments which ERASMUS students experienced at the host universities contrast or correspond to those prevailing at the home institution? To what extent do we observe characteristics of national systems of higher education in the European Community or a high degree of homogeneity? In order to explore these questions, students were asked to compare their home and their host university using 12 variables rated on a scale from 1 = "strongly emphasized" to 5 = "not at all emphasized". The list of variables was selected from a more extended list of items used in the above-mentioned survey conducted in the mid-eighties which had addressed participants of Joint Study Programmes, among others. The items referred to general cognitive dimensions, international dimensions of learning, teaching styles, modes of assessment, and finally modes of learning.

Firstly, the characteristics of higher education of the various EC Member States were described as viewed by students spending their ERASMUS supported period in that country. This was done in comparison with the pictures of higher education of that country provided by home students. The first two columns each in Table 5.5 serve as the bases for that comparison.

Higher education in the *Netherlands* was viewed by incoming ERASMUS students as most international, both in emphasizing comparative perspectives and the use of publications in foreign languages. Dutch students, however, did not perceive a strong emphasis on comparative perspectives at their home universities.

Germany was viewed by host students as a country in which the students' freedom and independence were strongly emphasized. Students had a high degree of freedom in choosing courses and areas and were expected to work independently. Little emphasis was placed on regular class attendance. Understanding theories, concepts and paradigms was highly appreciated. Assessment through written examinations and evaluation of papers submitted seemed to dominate. In slight contrast, German students believed that their home institutions emphasized a relatively strong role of the teachers as source of information and that evaluation of papers submitted played a much more limited role than written examinations.

Higher education in *Denmark* was viewed by incoming ERASMUS students in a similar way to higher education in Germany. This applied to students' freedom and independence as well as to a strong emphasis on theories. Evaluation of papers submitted seemed to play a role as well. Most marked contrasts between Danish and German higher education were, as seen by the foreign students, more out-of-class communication between teaching staff and students in Denmark as well as less emphasis on comparative perspectives. Danish students themselves found less freedom of choice at home; on the other hand, they strongly pointed out frequent use of publications in foreign languages at Danish universities.

United Kingdom universities were characterized by a strong emphasis on out-of-class communication between teaching staff and students, by an important role of evaluation of papers submitted, and by little use of publications in foreign languages. Students from other countries and British students were highly agreed in such perceptions.

Universities in *Ireland* were similarly viewed by foreign ERASMUS students to those in the United Kingdom. This applied to a strong emphasis on communication between teaching staff and students as well as little use of publications in foreign languages. Oral examinations, however, seemed to play a lesser role in Ireland. Irish students differed from foreign students in perceiving a stronger emphasis on theories in Irish higher education.

Universities in *France*, according to ERASMUS students going there, placed high emphasis on regular class attendance and on teachers as the main source of information. Little emphasis seemed to be placed on students' freedom of choice and autonomy or on out-of-class communication between teachers and students. French students pointed more strongly than foreign students to the role of written examinations in France and the acquisition of facts. In contrast to students from other countries, however, French students did not perceive a comparatively low emphasis on independent work of students in France.

Higher education in *Belgium* was viewed similarly to that in France by ERASMUS students from other countries in some respects, notably regarding emphasis on regular class attendance - a view not shared by Belgian students of their home universities - and little concern about out-of-class communication between teachers and students. Belgian students saw an even stronger emphasis on acquisition of facts in their home institutions than French students regarding French higher education. In contrast to France, however, host students in Belgium noted widespread use of publications in foreign languages as well as emphasis on oral examinations.

Higher education in *Portugal* was viewed by students from other countries as placing emphasis on regular class attendance and on teachers as the main source of information. Also similarly to France, Portuguese students noted a strong emphasis in Portugal on the acquisition of facts and on written examinations. In contrast to France, however, foreign ERASMUS students perceived a substantial use of literature in foreign languages in Portugal, and Portuguese students noted little emphasis in their home country on teachers as the main source of information.

Students spending the ERASMUS supported period in Spain noted the strong role of written examinations as well as little emphasis placed on students' freedom of choice and independent work. Spanish students, however, perceived some emphasis on theories and on independent work by students in Spain.

Italian universities emphasized according to the students' views, both understanding of theories and acquisition of facts. Students had little choice and were not highly expected to do independent work. Oral examinations were in the foreground and comparative perspectives were not strongly emphasized. In most respects, Italian universities were similarly viewed by foreign and Italian students, although the foreign students perceived (in contrast to Italian students) little emphasis placed on regular class attendance in Italy.

Foreign students reported a strong emphasis in Greece on comparative perspectives, little emphasis on acquisition of facts, and much out-of-class communication between teachers and students. Greek students, however, perceived exactly opposite characteristics of Greek higher education, i.e. strong emphasis on acquisition of facts, little concern about comparative perspectives, and little communication between teachers and students. In addition, home students pointed to a strong emphasis on the use of literature in foreign languages. It is not surprising to find that the strongest contrast between foreign and home students in perceiving characteristics of higher education was found in the case of Greece, because most ERASMUS students going there did not participate in regular course programmes at Greek universities, but rather in specific programmes for foreign students taught in a foreign language.

As a second step of analysis, it is possible to establish the extent to which students experienced similar or contrasting higher education milieus to those at home. In this case we compared the information provided from students of the respective countries on their home university and on the host university - irrespective of country they visited (the second and third columns each in Table 5.5).

Table 5.5a
Features of Academic Learning Climate at ERASMUS Students' Host and Home Universities, Assessed for Extent of Emphasis by Incoming and Outgoing (Home) Students, by Country (mean*)

	B univ. viewed by in-coming	B univ. viewed by out-going	B outgoing view on host univ.	D univ. viewed by in-coming	D univ. viewed by out-going	D outgoing view on host univ.	DK univ. viewed by in-coming	DK univ. viewed by out-going	DK outgoing view on host univ.
Acquiring facts	2.1	1.7	2.4	2.3	2.3	2.3	2.7	3.3	2.4
Understanding theories, concepts, paradigms	2.3	2.1	2.3	2.1	1.9	2.7	2.0	2.1	2.4
Providing comparative perspectives	2.3	2.6	2.7	2.5	2.8	2.7	3.1	3.1	3.1
Using publications in foreign languages	2.1	2.3	3.2	2.5	2.7	3.6	2.7	2.0	4.4
Regular class attendance	2.2	3.3	3.1	3.1	3.5	2.0	3.0	2.8	2.2
Teachers as the main source of information	2.2	2.6	2.9	3.1	2.4	2.0	3.1	2.9	2.3
Freedom to choose specific areas of study	2.8	3.2	2.3	2.1	2.4	3.3	2.0	2.6	3.4
Out-of class communication between students and teachers	3.2	3.5	2.4	2.9	3.5	2.6	2.1	2.5	3.2
Independent work	2.6	2.4	2.1	1.9	2.0	2.8	1.7	1.9	2.1
Oral examinations	1.8	1.8	2.7	2.8	3.1	3.0	2.9	2.9	3.5
Written examinations	2.9	2.9	2.8	1.9	1.8	1.8	2.8	1.9	1.7
Evaluation of papers submitted	2.3	2.4	2.4	2.1	2.9	2.4	2.3	2.1	2.1

Question 4.8: If you have taken regular courses at the host university together with host country students: According to your experience, to what extent are each of the following emphasized at your host university, as compared with your home university?

* On a scale from 1 = "strongly emphasized" to 5 = "not at all emphasized"

Table 5.5b
Features of Academic Learning Climate at ERASMUS Students' Host and Home Universities, Assessed for Extent of Emphasis by Incoming and Outgoing (Home) Students, by Country (mean*)

	E univ. viewed by in-coming	E univ. viewed by out-going	E outgoing view on host univ.	F univ. viewed by in-coming	F univ. viewed by out-going	F outgoing view on host univ.	GR univ. viewed by in-coming	GR univ. viewed by out-going	GR outgoing view on host univ.
Acquiring facts	2.1	2.5	3.0	2.2	1.9	2.3	2.9	2.1	2.2
Understanding theories, concepts, paradigms	2.6	2.1	2.3	2.6	2.0	2.2	2.4	2.0	1.8
Providing comparative perspectives	2.8	2.7	2.3	2.7	2.5	2.6	2.1	2.7	2.3
Using publications in foreign languages	3.2	2.7	2.7	3.1	2.7	3.2	3.3	2.4	3.2
Regular class attendance	2.6	2.5	2.4	2.1	2.4	3.0	2.7	3.0	2.0
Teachers as the main source of information	2.2	2.4	2.7	2.1	2.4	3.1	2.4	2.7	2.7
Freedom to choose specific areas of study	3.3	3.4	2.1	3.3	3.5	2.5	2.3	2.7	2.5
Out-of-class communication between students and teachers	2.8	2.9	2.8	3.5	3.3	2.1	2.1	2.9	2.6
Independent work	2.6	1.8	1.9	2.8	2.0	1.7	2.0	2.9	2.0
Oral examinations	3.3	3.5	2.5	2.6	2.6	3.0	3.3	2.8	3.0
Written examinations	1.7	1.4	2.2	1.8	1.5	1.7	2.4	1.6	1.6
Evaluation of papers submitted	2.5	2.5	1.9	2.5	2.1	2.1	2.2	2.6	2.0

Question 4.8: If you have taken regular courses at the host university together with host country students: According to your experience, to what extent are each of the following emphasized at your host university, as compared with your home university?

* On a scale from 1 = "strongly emphasized" to 5 = "not at all emphasized"

Table 5.5c
Features of Academic Learning Climate at ERASMUS Students' Host and Home Universities, Assessed for Extent of Emphasis by Incoming and Outgoing (Home) Students, by Country (mean*)

	I univ. viewed by in-coming	I univ. viewed by out-going	I outgoing view on host univ.	IRL univ. viewed by in-coming	IRL univ. viewed by out-going	IRL outgoing view on host univ.	NL univ. viewed by in-coming	NL univ. viewed by out-going	NL outgoing view on host univ.
Acquiring facts	1.8	2.1	2.4	2.4	2.2	2.7	2.6	2.4	2.2
Understanding theories, concepts, paradigms	2.1	1.8	2.3	2.6	1.5	1.9	2.4	2.3	2.6
Providing comparative perspectives	2.9	2.8	2.4	2.5	2.4	2.4	2.2	2.7	2.8
Using publications in foreign languages	3.2	2.8	2.8	3.6	4.0	2.9	2.0	2.3	3.6
Regular class attendance	2.8	2.4	1.9	2.8	2.5	2.9	2.6	3.3	2.8
Teachers as the main source of information	2.3	2.4	2.3	2.4	2.9	3.1	2.8	3.2	2.4
Freedom to choose specific areas of study	3.3	2.9	2.6	2.9	3.0	2.6	2.3	2.4	2.8
Out-of class communication between students and teachers	3.5	3.5	2.1	2.3	2.5	3.4	2.4	3.2	2.9
Independent work	2.6	3.6	2.5	2.3	1.8	2.4	2.1	2.0	2.5
Oral examinations	1.4	1.3	3.5	3.4	4.0	2.3	2.8	3.3	2.7
Written examinations	3.1	2.5	1.5	1.6	1.7	2.8	2.5	2.1	3.3
Evaluation of papers submitted	2.9	3.0	1.9	2.1	1.9	2.0	2.2	2.3	2.5

Question 4.8: If you have taken regular courses at the host university together with host country students: According to your experience, to what extent are each of the following emphasized at your host university, as compared with your home university?

* On a scale from 1 = "strongly emphasized" to 5 = "not at all emphasized"

Table 5.5d
Features of Academic Learning Climate at ERASMUS Students' Host and Home Universities, Assessed for Extent of Emphasis by Incoming and Outgoing (Home) Students, by Country (mean*)

	P univ. viewed by		P outgoing view on host univ.	UK univ. viewed by		UK outgoing view on host univ.
	in-coming	out-going		in-coming	out-going	
Acquiring facts	2.4	1.9	1.6	2.6	2.6	2.3
Understanding theories, concepts, paradigms	2.3	1.6	2.3	2.5	2.1	2.4
Providing comparative perspectives	2.9	2.4	1.8	2.7	2.5	2.8
Using publications in foreign languages	2.2	1.9	3.4	3.9	3.0	2.8
Regular class attendance	2.2	2.3	2.2	2.4	2.2	2.6
Teachers as the main source of information	2.1	3.0	2.0	2.8	3.1	2.5
Freedom to choose specific areas of study	3.6	3.4	2.1	2.7	2.8	3.3
Out-of class communication between students and teachers	2.6	2.7	2.1	2.1	2.3	4.0
Independent work	2.7	3.4	2.4	2.0	1.8	2.6
Oral examinations	3.0	3.0	2.4	3.4	3.2	2.6
Written examinations	2.5	1.1	2.2	1.8	1.7	2.0
Evaluation of papers submitted	2.3	2.5	2.0	2.0	1.9	2.5

Question 4.8: If you have taken regular courses at the host university together with host country students: According to your experience, to what extent are each of the following emphasized at your host university, as compared with your home university?

* On a scale from 1 = "strongly emphasized" to 5 = "not at all emphasized"

On average, the students reported substantial differences between higher education in their home and their host institutions. The differences perceived, according to the 12 aspects surveyed, were at least 0.9 and at most 1.6 points on the five-point-scale. This finding underscored the variety of higher education systems in the European Community with the largest perceived differences between the host and home institutions of higher education regarded as emphasis placed on:
- out-of-class communication between teachers and students (1.6)
- regular class attendance (1.5)
- oral examinations (1.5)
- use of publications in foreign languages (1.4)
- students' freedom to choose specific areas of study (1.4).

The perception of a strong emphasis on certain characteristics of higher education across all host institutions seemed to be an indirect indication of a respective weak emphasis felt at the home institutions. ERASMUS students described the contrasting experiences at home and abroad in the following ways:
- *French* students noted more freedom of choice and independent work abroad; they also experienced much less emphasis on regular class attendance in their respective host countries than in France.
- *Belgian* students perceived more freedom and independent work as well as more out-of-class communication at the host university than at home.
- *Spanish* students also noted more freedom of choice in specific areas at their host universities than at home, and reported more emphasis abroad on oral examinations and the evaluation of papers submitted.
- *Italian* students also experienced a stronger emphasis on independent learning abroad than at home. In contrast to Spain, however, they felt a stronger emphasis abroad on written examinations and on evaluation of papers submitted than in Italy, where oral examinations dominated. Italian students, finally, perceived more emphasis abroad than at home on out-of-class communication between teachers and students.
- *Portuguese* students noted a strong emphasis abroad on acquisition of facts, on comparative perspectives, on the teachers as a main source of information and on oral examinations. In addition, they perceived a stronger role of independent work at the host institution than at home. On the other hand, they found literature in foreign languages

less used abroad, and less out-of-class communication between teachers and students.
- *Greek* students reported a stronger emphasis on theories and independent work, but also on regular class attendance abroad. Also, the evaluation of papers submitted at host institutions seemed to be an uncommon experience for Greek students.
- *Danish* students perceived strong emphasis abroad on regular class attendance and on acquisition of facts.
- *German* students reported the same contrasts between host and home universities as Danish students did. In addition, German students pointed to less freedom of choice abroad and more emphasis abroad on out-of-class communication between teachers and students. Finally, they saw a stronger emphasis abroad on the evaluation of papers submitted.
- *British* students perceived less out-of-class communication abroad than at home as well as a stronger emphasis on the teacher as the main source of information.
- *Irish* students also pointed at lesser communication between teachers and students abroad. In addition, they experienced more use of publications in foreign languages and a stronger role of oral examinations at their host institutions than at home.
- *Dutch* students perceived more emphasis abroad on oral examinations and on the teacher as the main source of information. They observed at their host institutions less use of literature in foreign languages than they were accustomed to in the Netherlands.

5.4   Problems Faced during the Study Period Abroad

It is a matter of course that living and studying abroad posed not insignificant difficulties for students. In order to examine the extent to which problems occur, what major problems the students face, how they are related to certain programme settings, and to what extent they influenced the outcomes of the study period abroad, students were presented with a list of 19 possible problems. They were asked to state on a scale from 1 = "very serious problems" to 5 = "no problems at all", whether they had significant problems regarding:
- issues of living and organizing conditions of study in the host country (administrative matters, financial matters, guidance concerning non-

academic matters, accommodation, finding a place to concentrate on studies outside the classroom, not enough time available for travel)
- issues of study at the host university (academic level of courses, differences in the teaching and learning methods between home and host university, readiness on part of teaching staff to meet and help foreign students, differences in class or student project group size, guidance concerning academic programme)
- foreign language issues (taking courses in a foreign language, taking examinations in a foreign language, communication in a foreign language outside the classroom)
- issues regarding social contacts (interaction among/with host country students, not enough contact with people from the home country, too much contact with people from the home country)
- lifestyles of nationals in host country; and finally
- climate, food, health, etc.

Altogether, 58 percent of the ERASMUS students named problems of living and organizing the conditions of study in the host country, 34 percent mentioned problems of social contacts, 31 percent problems of study, and 20 percent stated foreign language problems. One fifth did not rate any of the 19 possible problems posed as serious (scale points 1 and 2). These aggregate percentages should be viewed with some caution because the numbers of items for each area differed.

As regards living and organizing conditions of study abroad, problems of accommodation were experienced by 22 percent of the ERASMUS students. Problems regarding administrative matters (21 %) and regarding financial matters (21 %) were reported almost equally often, as Table 5.6 shows. Less frequently problems were felt regarding a quiet place for self-study (13 %) and guidance on non-academic matters. In comparison with the students participating in Joint Study Programmes surveyed in the mid-eighties, the ERASMUS students reported less administrative problems, but somewhat more problems of accommodation (22 % as compared with 17 %), a quiet place for self-study and guidance regarding non-academic matters. As many ERASMUS students as JSP students stated problems of financial matters, although the JSP scheme - in contrast to the ERASMUS programme - did not provide financial support to students.

Table 5.6
Problems During Study Period Abroad, by Host Country (percentage*)

	Host country											Total
	B	D	DK	E	F	GR	I	IRL	NL	P	UK	
Taking courses in a foreign language	14	18	21	9	10	14	15	6	15	13	5	10
Taking examinations in a foreign language	9	25	17	8	18	10	21	9	15	8	11	15
Academic level of courses	12	15	8	8	9	5	12	5	4	3	4	8
Differences in teaching/learning betw. home and host university	14	16	11	22	24	10	28	7	11	20	12	17
Readiness of teachers to meet/help foreign students	11	20	7	15	27	9	29	3	8	15	4	15
Differences in class or student project group size	7	15	0	15	14	10	8	2	3	10	4	9
Administrative matters	17	27	21	22	30	7	45	6	11	29	9	21
Financial matters	21	21	20	29	21	12	34	17	14	24	19	21
Guidance concerning academic programme	16	20	11	24	26	15	36	10	10	27	8	18
Guidance concerning non-academic matters	13	9	7	17	18	10	24	3	8	18	4	12
Finding place to concentrate on studies outside class	4	5	10	21	17	12	26	19	5	45	9	13

(to be cont.)

(Table 5.6 cont.)

	B	D	DK	E	F	GR	I	IRL	NL	P	UK	Total
						Host country						
Accommodation	23	17	17	38	24	23	30	20	30	36	15	22
Climate, food, health etc.	5	4	0	7	7	9	5	16	3	3	15	9
Lifestyles of nationals in host country	7	2	3	4	5	5	4	8	6	3	8	5
Interaction among/with host country students	14	7	14	10	18	7	12	8	12	18	9	12
Not enough contact with people from your own country	4	3	3	2	4	2	5	3	5	0	4	4
Too much contact with people from your own country	18	25	14	19	29	24	23	25	13	21	31	26
Communicating in foreign language outside the class	7	8	21	4	8	23	8	5	14	24	6	8
Not enough time available for travel	12	18	14	18	21	9	19	12	16	30	25	20

Question 6.1: To what extent did you have significant problems in any of the following areas during your study period abroad?

* Percent 1 + 2 on a scale from 1 = "very serious problems" to 5 = "no problems at all"

Financial problems as well as problems of accommodation are discussed in Chapters 6 and 7. Administrative problems were by far most often faced by ERASMUS students in Italy (45 %) followed by those who had spent their study period in France (30 %), Portugal (29 %) and the Federal Republic of Germany (27 %); least administrative problems were reported by students who went to Ireland (6 %), Greece (7 %) and the United Kingdom (9 %). Conversely, Irish (41 %) and British students (40 %) were much more frequently confronted with problems in administrative matters abroad. Certainly, support in administrative matters by the host university turned out to be very limited in some countries. In addition, students coming from countries in which universities tended to provide support to their students in non-academic matters were most disappointed about the limited support in administrative matters abroad.

As regards academic matters, few students felt problems regarding the academic level of courses at host universities (8 %). Problems regarding guidance on academic matters (18 %), differences in teaching and learning styles (17 %) and regarding the readiness of teachers to meet and help students (15 %) were most often stated. Differences in the teaching and learning styles were less often seen as problems by ERASMUS students than by JSP students.

The frequency of academic problems reported varied markedly by host country and home country. Most academic problems were felt by students who spent their study period abroad in:

- Italy (23 % on average regarding the five aspects surveyed as compared with 13 percent on average of all countries); in comparison with other countries, guidance on academic matters and readiness on the part of teachers to meet and help students was especially missed at Italian universities
- France (20 %) caused the second highest level of academic problems to incoming students. Notably, lack of readiness on part of the teachers to meet and help students was frequently reported.
- Students going to Germany (17 % on average reported problems) had problems relatively often concerning the academic level of courses (15 %), while students going to Spain (17 %) referred over-proportionally to differences in class size (15 %).
- Students who went to Ireland, the United Kingdom, the Netherlands, and Denmark reported very few academic problems (5-7 % on average on the various aspects).

As regards home country, we note that British (28 % on average) and Irish students (20 %) reported problems higher than average on academic issues abroad than students from all other countries (7-13 % respectively). More frequently, they had problems not only regarding contacts, class size, guidance and teaching and learning styles (the latter only in the case of British students), but also more problems related to the academic level of courses at the host institution. As British and Irish students did not report less academic progress abroad in comparison to that at home than did German and Danish students, these findings suggest that British and Irish students faced problems with the educational environments abroad putting less emphasis on contacts between teachers and students and on good teaching practice. Fortunately, this experience led to low academic achievement in a limited number of cases.

Fifteen percent of the ERASMUS students who were taught abroad mostly in a foreign language reported significant problems as regards taking examinations in a foreign language. Taking courses in that language (10 %) and communication in a foreign language outside the classroom (8 %) posed problems least often. Difficulties in taking examinations in a foreign language were most often stated by students who went to the Federal Republic of Germany (25 %) and to Italy, with Irish (35 %) and Danish students (25 %) the visitors who reported these problems most often.

Fewer students going abroad for at most six months (12 %) reported problems in taking examinations abroad than those going abroad for a longer period (17 %). This is certainly unexpected at first glance, since the foreign language proficiency, as rated by the students themselves, seemed to grow with the duration of the study period abroad. Problems of communicating in the foreign language outside the classroom were stated by 23 percent of students going abroad for less than three months, 11 percent for those going abroad for three months, seven percent for those going abroad for about six months, and six percent of those going abroad for more than six months. Obviously, however, students going abroad for more than six months were more likely to be involved in taking examinations in a foreign language. Correspondingly, problems regarding the academic level of courses abroad seemed more likely to be felt the longer the study period abroad: five percent among those going abroad for at most three months as compared with 10 percent among those going abroad for more than six months. It seemed that a serious immersion into the academic life at the host university only occurred if the study period abroad lasted at least three months and that study and examinations abroad were more demanding if the study period at the host university lasted about one academic year.

Many ERASMUS students disliked the many contacts with people from their own country. This was notably felt by students of those ICPs sending large numbers of students abroad. Some of the positive effects of a more systematic support and of curricular coordination of large programmes seemed to stem from the fact that students going abroad together with fellow students from the same department tended to stick together and thus limit exposure to the host environment. Problems of interaction among or with host country students were reported by 12 percent of the respondents, notably those going to France and Portugal (18 % each).

Few difficulties were felt regarding the lifestyles of host country nationals or the climate, food, etc. abroad. The former problems were most often stated by Greek students (19 % as compared with 5 % among all ERASMUS students), the latter most often by Portuguese (30 %) and Greek students (28 % as compared with 9 % among all ERASMUS students).

5.5   Integration into the Academic and Social Life of Students at the Host University

As to the extent to which they felt integrated into the academic life and into the social life of students at the host university, students replied in a cautiously positive way. On a scale from 1 = "to a great extent" to 5 = "not at all", the mean ratings were both 2.5. As Chart 5.2 shows, the ratings were higher the longer the period abroad lasted; they ranged from 2.8 in the case of stays of 1-2 months, to 2.0 or 2.1 in the case of students staying abroad for more than one year.

ERASMUS students felt most integrated in the United Kingdom, Ireland and Germany, as the section on the left of Chart 5.3 shows. The differences of integration felt according to host country were neither clearly linked to the average duration of stays in those countries nor to the extent of instruction in the language of the host country. They seemed to be most clearly associated with proficiency in the host country language outside the classroom.

Chart 5.2
Integration into Academic and Social Life in the Host Country, by Duration of the Study Period Abroad (mean)

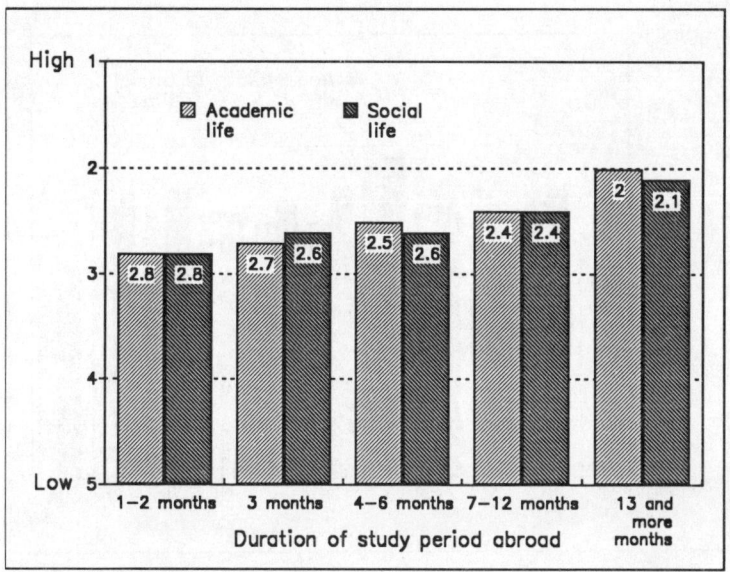

French students felt integrated to the highest extent in the academic life of the host institutions (2.1), while British students felt academically least integrated (3.1). As regards social integration, a similar pattern can be observed, as the section on the right of Chart 5.3 shows, though the difference was somewhat smaller (2.2 and 2.8). It seems that the level of expectations varies among students from different countries: as British universities seemed to foster communication both among students and between teachers and students most strongly, British students seemed to expect a high degree of communication abroad and therefore negatively rated the setting abroad; although they might have had more problems in communicating abroad. Conversely, French students who experienced little communication at the home institution might have perceived foreign higher education milieus more favourable to integration, or they might in fact more easily get integrated into the academic or social life of host institutions.

Chart 5.3
Integration into Academic and Social Life in the Host Country, by Host Country and Country of Home University (mean)

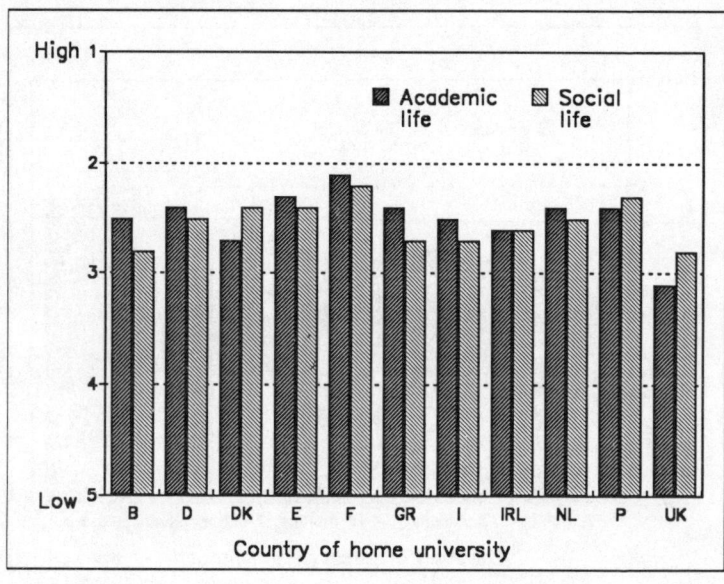

Country of home university

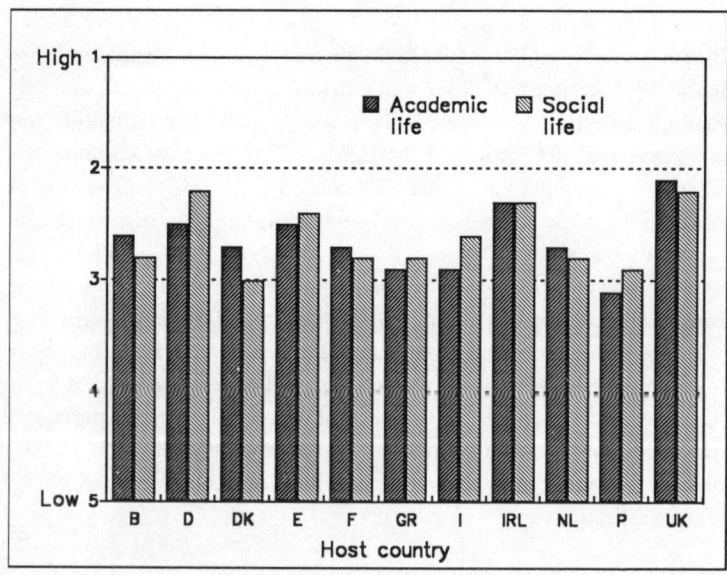

Host country

Chapter 6

Accommodation in the Host Country

6.1 Introduction

The rapid increase in the number of students spending a period of study in another country of the European Community has led to concern about the accommodation of mobile students. Some experts claim that a further extension of mobility could not be envisaged unless serious efforts were made to provide additional student housing. Notably, problems regarding students' search for accommodation and the quality of housing are reported from metropolitan areas of the EC[1].

In view of this debate, the survey of the experiences of 1988/89 ERASMUS students went into greater detail on accommodation than on other issues. Notably, attention was paid to the search period, the quality of housing, the information offered on accommodation, and proposals for improvement of accommodation of ERASMUS students.

It should be added that the student survey is only suitable to show part of the accommodation problems, i.e. those experienced by the students themselves. For example, whether accommodation was at hand upon arrival, what role other students played, what experiences they had when searching for accommodation, and problems they noted regarding the room, apartment or house where they lived while studying at the host university. Information on one of the problems most often referred to will have to be traced from other persons, that is the efforts made and

---

1   Cf. also E. Berning in cooperation with M. Weihrich-Dunkel and W. Fischer. Accommodation of ERASMUS-Students in the Member States of the European Community. München: Bayerisches Staatsinstitut für Hochschulforschung und Hochschulplanung, 1990, mimeo.

the problems encountered by the universities themselves in providing accommodation for incoming ERASMUS students.

6.2   Main Modes of Accommodation in Home and Host Country

About half of the students supported by the ERASMUS programme were provided with university accommodation (halls of residences furnished by universities or other agencies for the accommodation of students) during the study period at the host university. As Table 6.1 shows, about a third of the students had an apartment or house abroad which they shared with other students, while about one tenth had lived in a room in a private home. Other modes of accommodation played hardly any role. In addition, it should be pointed out that the question posed allowed for various kinds of accommodation and if the students had moved during their period abroad; in fact, eight percent of the students named two categories of accommodation.

The proportion of students provided with university accommodation varies strongly according to host country:
- the majority of ERASMUS students going to the United Kingdom and the Federal Republic of Germany (65 % each) and those going to France (59 %) lived in halls of residence
- almost half of the students spending their study period abroad in Denmark and Italy (48 % each) lived in halls of residence
- the proportion of ERASMUS students going to Greece and Belgium who lived in university accommodation (38 % each) was not higher than those living in apartments or houses together with other students. It must be added that more students going to Greece lived in hotels or pensions (26 %) than students going to other countries
- students going to the Netherlands and Portugal were twice as likely to live in an apartment or room with other students than in university halls of residence (29 % and 24 % respectively)
- few students going to Spain (17 %) and Ireland (9 %) lived in university halls of residence during their study abroad period. Apartments or houses together with other students or rooms with private families were more common or at least as frequent as university accommodation.

Table 6.1

Accommodation During Study at Host University, by Host University (percentage)

	Host country											Total
	B	D	DK	E	F	GR	I	IRL	NL	P	UK	
University accommodation	38	65	48	17	59	38	47	9	29	24	65	52
Apartment/house together with other students	35	21	39	61	28	40	39	51	49	49	32	35
Own apartment/flat	2	2	0	2	2	0	2	3	3	0	0	2
Apartment/house with parents/relatives	2	2	3	1	0	0	1	4	1	0	0	1
Apartment/house with partner and/or children	2	1	0	3	1	0	1	2	1	5	1	1
Room in private home with another family	9	11	6	17	9	0	2	35	10	17	8	10
Hotel/pension/boarding house	11	2	6	12	4	26	12	3	4	12	2	5
Other	3	4	3	2	3	0	3	5	9	0	1	3
Total	102	107	106	113	107	105	109	111	105	107	109	108
(n)	(94)	(371)	(32)	(314)	(849)	(43)	(210)	(109)	(188)	(41)	(961)	(3212)

Question 5.1: Where did you live most of the time during your studies at your home university and during the study period abroad?

Students were also asked about their accommodation while studying at home. As Table 6.2 shows, only 19 percent lived in student halls of residence while studying at home, 30 percent lived in apartments and houses together with other students - exactly the same proportion as during the study period abroad and 30 percent lived at their parents' or relatives' apartment or house. Thus, we note that slightly more ERASMUS students lived in university accommodation abroad than the total who lodged in university accommodation and with parents and relatives while studying at home.

Again, differences of accommodation while studying at home varied substantially by home country. Students from the United Kingdom (33 %), Denmark (29 %), Germany (23 %) and France (20 %) most often lived in halls of residence while studying at home - i.e. with the exception of Italy (7 %), those countries in which universities succeeded in 1988/89 in providing university accommodation for about half or even more of the incoming ERASMUS students.

It might be added that the largest proportions of Irish, British, Belgian, Dutch and German students shared apartments or houses with other students while studying at home. On the other hand, many Spanish, Italian, Greek, Portuguese and French students lived with their parents and relatives while studying in their home country.

The type of accommodation abroad was to some extent linked to the duration of the study abroad period, as Chart 6.1 shows:

- the longer the duration of the study period abroad, the higher the percentage of students who lived in university halls of residence; 60 percent of those abroad for more than half a year as compared to 42 percent of those abroad for at most two months
- an exception in this respect were those students staying abroad supported by the ERASMUS programme for more than one year. Most of them lived in apartments or houses together with other students
- a quarter of all students spending at most two months abroad lived in hotels or pensions during this period (as compared to 5 % of all ERASMUS students on average).

Table 6.2
Accommodation During Study at Home University, by Country of Home University (percentage)

	B	D	DK	E	F	GR	I	IRL	NL	P	UK	Total
					Country of home university							
University accommodation	9	23	29	7	20	5	7	5	8	0	33	19
Apartment/house together with other students	51	33	19	22	24	8	27	64	48	10	61	36
Apartment/house with parents/relatives	31	21	5	67	36	57	61	31	18	50	6	30
Apartment/house with partner and/or children	2	8	24	1	7	3	3	0	6	10	4	5
Room in private home with another family	7	8	12	1	11	3	3	0	4	30	3	6
Hotel/pension/boarding house	1	0	0	1	1	3	2	0	0	0	0	1
Own appartement/flat	0	6	0	0	3	19	1	0	7	0	2	3
Home - other	3	5	14	1	3	3	1	5	12	0	0	3
Total	104	104	102	101	105	100	104	105	102	100	109	105
(n)	(211)	(745)	(42)	(303)	(632)	(37)	(276)	(39)	(151)	(10)	(585)	(3031)

Question 5.1: Where did you live most of the time during your studies at your home university and during the study period abroad?

Chart 6.1
Type of Accommodation Abroad, by Duration of Study Period Abroad
(percentage)

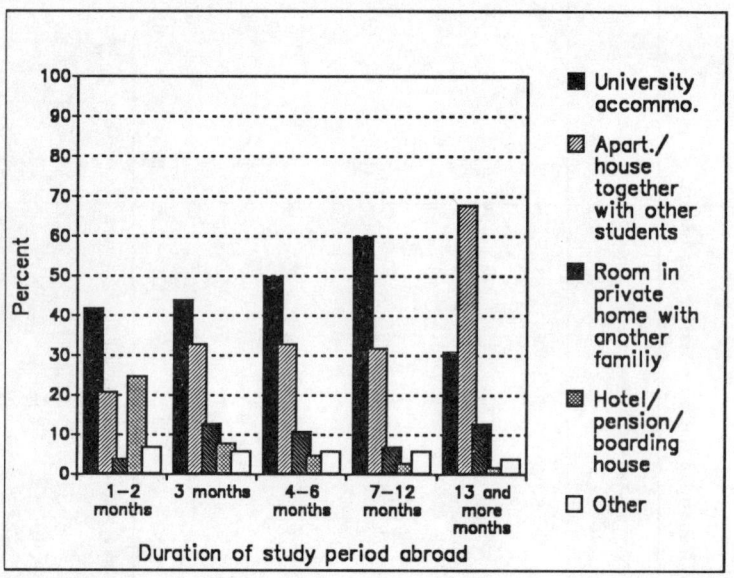

6.2   Change of Accommodation Abroad

The majority of students (61 %) stayed for the whole study period abroad in the same accommodation, 21 percent moved once, and 18 percent twice or even more often. On average, students had 1.7 homes during their study period abroad. The frequency of change of accommodation varied according to the duration of the study period abroad to a lesser extent than one might have expected. For example, 39 percent of those staying abroad for more than half a year moved at least once compared with 34 percent of those staying abroad for three months; however, those staying abroad less than two months moved less often. As already noted, accommodation in pensions and hotels helped in avoiding moves during such a short period. On the other hand, 80 percent of those staying abroad for more than one year moved more than once - half of them twice or more.

Change of accommodation during the study period abroad was most often reported by students going to Ireland and Spain - i.e. those countries in which university accommodation was least often provided for ERASMUS students. In general, we note that living in university halls of residence was the most stable form of accommodation. Those living there moved during their study abroad period half as often (26 %) as students who did not live in university accommodation abroad (52 %).

Around 30 percent of the students who participated in work placement abroad had to change accommodation, because the location of the work placement was far away from that of the host institution. This explains almost one tenth of all changes of accommodation during the study abroad period reported by all ERASMUS students. Those participating in work placement abroad moved 2.4 times on average, in other words, 1.4 times in addition to moves caused by the distance of location between work place and host university.

In fact, more than half (57 %) of the students who moved during the study abroad period - 22 percent of all ERASMUS students - intended to do so from the beginning. Moves caused by the fact that students got provisional accommodation for a few days or weeks accounted for more than a third of all changes of accommodation abroad reported by the ERASMUS students.

The average duration of temporary arrangements for accommodation was 32 days:
- 6 days on average in those cases in which the total ERASMUS-supported period abroad lasted at most two months
- 17 days in those cases in which the total period abroad lasted three months
- 22 days in the cases where the total period abroad was 4-6 months
- 40 days if the total period abroad was 7-12 months.

Of all students facing temporary accommodation arrangements at the beginning, 48 percent moved to regular accommodation within two weeks and a further 35 percent within one month. 18 percent of those facing temporary arrangements (4 % of all students responding) had to wait longer than a month before they could move to a regular home.

A survey on accommodation of foreign students in the United Kingdom conducted in 1988/89 showed that 30 percent of the students surveyed had temporary arrangements at the beginning of their stay in the United Kingdom[2], i.e. a larger proportion than the respective one among all ERASMUS students surveyed (22 %) or among ERASMUS students going to the United Kingdom (19 %). More than one third of the foreign students in the United Kingdom who spent some period in temporary arrangements had to stay there for more than one month compared with 18 percent of all ERASMUS students facing temporary arrangements and 24 percent of ERASMUS students facing temporary arrangements in the United Kingdom. These findings support the widely held view that on average other foreign students face more serious accommodation problems than ERASMUS students.

Change of accommodation during the study period abroad cannot be considered a phenomenon exclusively attributable to problems of accommodation abroad. For students also change accommodation while studying at home - in some cases because of unsatisfactory living conditions at the previous location, in other cases for various personal reasons. Those students who had studied at least a year prior to the ERASMUS supported period abroad were therefore asked how frequently they had changed their accommodation during their first year of study at their home institution. 15 percent of the respondents had changed accommodation once during the first year of study at home, and a further five percent twice or more. Notably, many Danish students had moved during their first year of study (35 %), compared to few Spanish (5 %) and Belgian students (7 %).

Thus, students studying abroad were 3 times as likely to move during the study period compared with their first year of study at home, even though the study period abroad was usually shorter than one year (7 months). Even if we did not take into consideration the moves during the study period abroad, which were intended to be temporary from the beginning, the remaining changes of accommodation abroad happened about twice as often as during one year at the home institution. Thus, more than half of the changes of accommodation during the study period abroad were due to the specific conditions of studying abroad.

---

2   R. Hughes. *Homes Far from Home*. London: Overseas Students Trust, 1990, p. 14.

6.3   Provision of Accommodation and Time Span for Search

As already mentioned in Chapter 4, ERASMUS students were asked what kind of assistance and advice they were given by the host university and how satisfied they were with the assistance provided. 52 percent of the students rated the extent of assistance and advice regarding accommodation as "substantial" and 30 percent as "modest", while 18 percent reported no assistance in this respect (see Table 4.6).

In two host countries, far less assistance and advice regarding accommodation was provided than in all other countries:

- 48 percent of the students who went to Spain obtained no assistance and advice on accommodation, 35 percent reported modest, and only 17 percent substantial support
- in Portugal, 31 percent of the incoming ERASMUS students had no assistance and advice, 38 percent modest and 31 percent substantial support as regards accommodation.

Altogether, the findings in Chapter 4 provided evidence that the degree of satisfaction expressed by students was closely linked to the amount of assistance perceived. As regards accommodation, when students perceived a relatively high degree of assistance, they expressed a relatively high degree of satisfaction (2.6 on average on a scale from 1 = "very high" to 5 = "very low"). The support provided in Denmark, Germany and the United Kingdom was rated most positively (2.2 each) - three countries in which a large proportion of students were provided university accommodation. In the case of two other countries frequently providing university accommodation, however, (France and Italy) students were on average less satisfied with the support provided (2.8 each). As one could expect from the findings reported above, assistance provided regarding accommodation was most negatively rated by students who had spent their study abroad period in Spain (3.6); no host country was rated worse as regards any of the 13 aspects of assistance and support which were addressed in the respective question. Also assistance regarding housing provided in Portugal was rated clearly more negatively (3.2) than that in the remaining countries.

Asked in more detail about the role of the host university (staff as well as students) in finding accommodation:

- 57 percent of ERASMUS students reported that regular accommodation was provided

- 8 percent were provided with temporary accommodation;
- 15 percent at least had assistance for their own search for accommodation;
- 11 percent reported that they had no support regarding accommodation; and
- 10 percent had their own accommodation arrangements, and had therefore informed the university that they did not need any support.

According to the survey referred to above, 61 percent of the foreign students in the United Kingdom found accommodation by means of institutional assistance and one percent through the student union[3]. 60 percent of the ERASMUS students (61 % of those going to the United Kingdom) reported support in finding accommodation, but some of them had no support by the institutional staff and for an unknown proportion, this support was not essential in finding accommodation. There it seems justified to assume that more ERASMUS students than other foreign students were expected to be active themselves in the search for accommodation.

As Table 6.3 shows, regular accommodation was provided by the host university (with the help of staff and students) for:
- about 70 percent of the ERASMUS students going to Denmark
- about 60 percent of those going to Belgium, Germany, France, Italy, the Netherlands, the United Kingdom, and Portugal
- 46 percent of those going to Greece and 30 percent of those going to Ireland
- 23 percent of those going to Spain.

One should add that Portuguese universities provided accommodation for an average proportion of incoming students. The criticism as regards limited support noted above obviously reflects the fact that no help was given by Portuguese universities for those guest students who were not provided with accommodation and who had to search for it themselves.

As Table 6.3 indicates, students of the host university played some role in finding accommodation for the incoming ERASMUS students; they found regular accommodation in seven percent of the cases and temporary accommodation for two percent of the guest students. A further 12 percent of the students reported other kinds of help by the

---

3   Hughes 1990, p. 146.

Table 6.3
Role of Staff and Students in Finding Accommodation, by Host Country (percentage)

	Host country											Total
	B	D	DK	E	F	GR	I	IRL	NL	P	UK	
Staff: regular accomm.	45	52	63	15	48	42	57	17	37	38	54	46
Stud.: regular accomm.	10	6	3	7	19	2	5	10	15	10	3	7
Staff and students: regular accomm.	5	5	3	1	3	2	3	6	7	8	3	4
Staff: temporary accomm.	10	6	7	10	5	16	7	16	5	8	4	6
Stud.: temporary accomm.	1	3	0	3	2	2	0	1	3	3	1	2
Staff and students: temporary accomm.	0	0	3	0	0	0	0	1	1	0	1	0
Staff: assistance	7	7	7	8	6	7	6	25	6	3	7	7
Students: assistance	11	3	0	11	5	5	2	3	3	3	3	5
Staff and stud.: assistance	2	2	0	4	2	5	0	5	9	0	3	3
No support	2	9	7	27	11	9	10	5	5	28	8	11
Own arrangements	7	7	7	14	9	9	10	11	9	0	13	10
Total	100	100	100	100	100	100	100	100	100	100	100	100
(n)	(91)	(359)	(30)	(301)	(822)	(43)	(205)	(106)	(182)	(39)	(913)	(3091)

Question 5.6: What role did the host university staff and students play in finding your accommodation?

host university students: finding accommodation in cooperation with the university staff or assisting the incoming students in their own search.

Host universities, as a rule, most easily can help the ERASMUS students in providing university accommodation. Of those ERASMUS students, however, who eventually did not live in university accommodation during their study abroad period:
- 35 percent were provided with accommodation through the help of host university staff and students
- 12 percent were provided with temporary accommodation
- 23 percent were provided with assistance for their own search
- 15 percent had no support
- 15 percent made their own arrangements.

ERASMUS students spent on average 10.5 hours searching for accommodation. Of this time, 6.3 hours were spent in finding first accommodation, and 4.2 hours for finding subsequent accommodation, when students either had to move or decided themselves to move.

Table 6.4
Hours Spent Altogether on Finding Accomodation Abroad, by Host Country
(percentage)

	Host country											Total
	B	D	DK	E	F	GR	I	IRL	NL	P	UK	
None	72	78	94	44	67	58	76	46	75	68	71	68
1 - 5 hours	11	8	0	6	9	14	2	11	9	2	8	8
6 - 10 hours	8	3	0	9	5	7	5	14	5	2	5	5
11 - 20 hours	3	4	6	13	7	7	7	14	3	2	6	7
21 - 30 hours	1	2	0	10	3	2	1	5	5	7	3	3
31 - 40 hours	2	2	0	4	2	5	1	2	1	2	2	2
41 and more	3	4	0	14	9	7	7	9	2	15	5	7
Total	100	100	100	100	100	100	100	100	100	100	100	100
(n)	(93)	(370)	(32)	(314)	(848)	(43)	(210)	(109)	(188)	(41)	(961)	(3209)

Question 5.7: About how many hours did you spend on searching before you had finally secured your first regular accommodation in the host country? If you looked for additional accommodation, how many hours did you spend altogether on finding accommodation?

The time spent on search was quite unevenly distributed, as Table 6.4 shows with 68 percent of the students stating that they did not spend any time searching for accommodation. This proportion is somewhat higher than one would expect, because only 56 percent reported accommodation provided by the host university and a further 11 percent had made their own arrangements in advance.

20 percent of the ERASMUS students reported that they spent up to 20 hours in finding accommodation, a further five percent up to 40 hours, and seven percent more than 40 hours. Again, differences according to host country were remarkable, from students going to Denmark who spent one hour on average on the search for accommodation to those going to Spain who spent 21 hours.

Only 59 percent of the students could move directly into a regular room or other kind of accommodation upon arrival: 41 percent had to spend a waiting time, as Table 6.5 shows, 24 percent had to wait for up to one week, and three percent for over one month. In two countries, Spain (73 %) and Ireland (72 %), the majority of incoming students had no regular accommodation upon arrival. Most students going to Ireland were provided with or found regular accommodation within a week; however, the proportion of those not being in regular accommodation within one week after arrival was 37 percent of those studying in Spain and 24 percent of those studying in Portugal, compared with 7 - 17 percent in the remaining countries.

As reported in section 6.2, 22 percent of the students stated that they had stayed in accommodation which was intended to be temporary. The findings suggest that an additional fifth of the students spent a few days upon arrival in hotels, with friends or in rooms vacated for a few days etc., not considered to be temporary "accommodation".

Of those who had university accommodation, 75 percent could move in directly upon arrival, 15 percent had to wait up to one week, and ten percent more than one week. Only 42 percent of those not provided with university accommodation could, immediately upon arrival, move into a regular room or an apartment. A quarter of them had to wait more than a week.

In summary, 59 percent of the ERASMUS students could move into a room or an apartment upon arrival. In about two thirds of these cases the host university (mostly its staff and in some cases its students) had provided the accommodation; in about one sixth of the cases, the incoming students had made arrangements in advance, and in about a further sixth of the cases, the immediate availability of rooms remains unexplained by the data provided in the questionnaire.

Table 6.5
Days Between Arrival and Finding Accommodation, by Host Country
(percentage)

	Host Country											Total
	B	D	DK	E	F	GR	I	IRL	NL	P	UK	
None	71	71	56	27	59	49	61	28	72	56	64	59
1 - 7 days	17	15	34	36	24	42	24	57	12	20	21	24
8 - 14 days	4	4	9	18	5	2	4	11	4	10	7	7
15 - 30 days	4	6	0	14	9	7	7	3	9	12	5	7
31 and more	3	4	0	5	3	0	5	1	4	2	3	3
Total	100	100	100	100	100	100	100	100	100	100	100	100
(n)	(93)	(370)	(32)	(314)	(848)	(43)	(210)	(109)	(188)	(41)	(961)	(3209)

Question 5.8: How many days passed between your arrival in the host country and finding your first regular accommodation?

Of those 41 percent not moving into an apartment or a room immediately upon arrival, a further nine percent received enough help so that they did not have to seek accommodation themselves. The remaining 32 percent spent on average more than ten hours on the search for accommodation. The time span between arrival and first regular accommodation was on average six days for all students, or 14 days on average for those not immediately moving into regular accommodation. Slightly more than half of those not moving into an apartment or a room immediately upon arrival reported that their accommodation initially was intended to be temporary, whereas others found some ways of living during the first days which they would not call "temporary accommodation". 24 percent had their regular accommodation within one week after arrival, a further 14 percent needed more than a week but less than a month, and for three percent it was more than a month before they finally had a regular room or an apartment in the host country.

6.4 Problems Encountered in Search for Accommodation

Almost all the 44 percent of ERASMUS students who had to seek accommodation in the host country themselves - with or without assistance from the host university - faced some difficulties they considered worth mentioning.

The three problems most often noted refer to the housing market:
- expensive accommodation (27 %)
- scarcity of accommodation (25 %)
- poor quality of available accommodation (19 %).

The fourth most often stated problem was also related to the housing market, although in a specific context; 13 percent reported that most of the accommodation available was too far away from the university or too inconveniently located in general.

Problems related to the foreign students' difficulties in searching for accommodation were mentioned much less often, though they cannot be considered marginal:
- they did not know where and how to look (12 %)
- they had language difficulties (8 %).

Finally, problems of finding accommodation were less often noted due to owners' or landlords' specific reservations against the students searching for accommodation:
- some owners, landlords, etc. did not like students (6 %)
- difficulties because of nationality, religion or colour (4 %)
- difficulties because of sex (1 %).

Other difficulties were mentioned by six percent of the students.
In general, though not in all cases, more problems were stated on average by students going to those countries in which university accommodation was only provided for a minority of ERASMUS students. For example:
- ERASMUS students searching for accommodation in Belgium and the Netherlands faced relatively few problems
- students seeking accommodation in Ireland notably criticized the poor quality of rooms or apartments offered; accommodation offered in Spain was criticised for the same reason. Students going to both countries stated inconvenient location relatively often as a problem

they encountered
- too expensive accommodation was mentioned most often by students who spent the period abroad in Spain, Italy and Greece
- scarcity of accommodation was most frequently mentioned by students going to Spain, Portugal and Greece
- reservations on the part of the owners, landlords etc. against students in general or due to nationality or sex of the students were most frequently experienced in Spain, but also relatively frequently in France, although many students going to France did not have to seek for accommodation themselves
- difficulties because of language and because students did not know where and how to look were most often stated by students going to Greece, Spain and Portugal.

Table 6.6
Problems Encountered in Search for Accommodation Abroad, by Host Country (percentage)

| | \multicolumn{11}{c}{Host country} | Total |
	B	D	DK	E	F	GR	I	IRL	NL	P	UK	
Did not know where and how to look	12	10	6	25	13	23	15	15	13	17	6	12
Had language difficulties	3	7	0	16	8	23	11	6	9	24	5	8
Accommodation was scarce	13	27	13	48	24	19	32	21	27	34	17	25
Quality of accommodation available was mostly poor	19	6	13	35	15	21	12	46	15	17	22	19
Acc. available too far from univ., inconv. located	6	7	13	24	12	7	15	30	9	17	13	13
Accomm. was expensive	7	15	19	50	25	33	34	27	27	24	26	27
Too busy studying etc.	1	3	0	4	3	0	5	3	5	2	2	3
Some owners/landlords etc. did not like students	4	6	3	11	8	5	6	5	3	0	4	6
Difficulties because of nationality/religion/colour	4	3	0	8	6	0	4	1	2	2	1	4
Difficulties because of sex	1	1	0	5	1	0	1	2	0	0	1	1
Other	5	5	0	10	6	7	8	10	3	2	5	6
Not ticked	62	65	75	26	58	51	55	34	57	49	61	56
Total	138	156	141	262	179	188	199	198	169	190	161	179
(n)	(94)	(371)	(32)	(314)	(849)	(43)	(210)	(109)	(188)	(41)	(961)	(3212)

Question 5.9: What problems did you face in the search for accommodation? (multiple reply possible)

6.5   Quality of Accommodation

Altogether, 1988/89 ERASMUS students were not dissatisfied with their accommodation in the host country. On average, they rated 2.6 on a scale from 1 = "very good" to 5 = "very bad". They considered accommodation abroad, however, clearly worse than accommodation at home which was rated 1.8 on average. 22 percent of the ERASMUS students rated their accommodation abroad as bad (scale points 4 and 5), but only five percent did so on accommodation at home.

Table 6.7
Quality of Accommodation in Host Country and in Home Country (percentage)

	B	D	DK	E	F	GR	I	IRL	NL	P	UK	Total
In host country,												
viewed by host students												
1 = very good	18	39	42	16	9	12	22	12	22	22	17	18
2	20	32	45	35	26	30	32	25	31	41	28	29
3	46	21	10	30	33	35	26	32	30	24	33	31
4	11	5	3	15	23	12	14	26	12	7	17	16
5 = very bad	4	2	0	4	10	12	5	6	5	5	5	6
Total	100	100	100	100	100	100	100	100	100	100	100	100
(n)	(93)	(364)	(31)	(313)	(842)	(43)	(208)	(109)	(183)	(41)	(954)	(3181)
In country of home university												
viewed by home students												
1 = very good	48	39	40	55	47	57	62	52	31	44	30	43
2	37	43	44	28	32	30	22	38	48	22	41	36
3	10	15	14	11	15	5	13	10	15	33	24	16
4	4	3	2	4	5	5	3	0	5	0	5	4
5 = very bad	1	0	0	2	1	3	1	0	1	0	1	1
Total	100	100	100	100	100	100	100	100	100	100	100	100
(n)	(214)	(756)	(43)	(301)	(639)	(37)	(279)	(40)	(153)	(9)	(608)	(3079)

Question 5.11: How would you, in general, describe the quality of your accommodation in the host country and in your home country?

Greek (1.7:3.1). German (1.8:3.1), Danish (1.8:3.0) and Italian students (1.6:2.7) rated accommodation while studying at home far better than accommodation abroad, whereas Portuguese (1.9:2.1) and British students (2.1:2.5) viewed accommodation abroad as only slightly inferior.

Two host countries clearly stood out in the quality of accommodation provided. As Table 6.7 shows, 87 percent of ERASMUS students studying for some period in Denmark rated housing provided there as good; they considered it better than accommodation in their respective home countries. Accommodation was viewed second best in the Federal Republic of Germany, where 71 percent of the host students rated it as good; this matches more or less the quality of accommodation students going to Germany had when studying in their respective home countries. As regards the remaining countries, positive ratings ranged from 35 to 63 percent, with accommodation in France (33 % negative ratings) and Ireland (32 % negative ratings) being considered worst, and differences from accommodation in their home country largest.

About 79 percent of the ERASMUS students stated that they had problems with the quality of their principal accommodation in the host country.

The range of problems faced was obviously broad: the most frequent one was stated by 29 percent of the students, compared with nine percent for the problem least frequently mentioned. Small size of the room as well as problems of furniture and equipment were most frequently mentioned, with problems in sharing facilities with others as well as noise or rude treatment by neighbours following closely, as Table 6.8 shows. As regards host countries, we might point out the following patterns:

- the relatively high standard of accommodation provided to ERASMUS students in Denmark can be demonstrated by the facts that, first, 41 percent of those studying in Denmark did not mention any problems at all (compared with 21 percent of all ERASMUS students) and second, the problem most often mentioned was that of inconvenient location as regards the host university
- the quality of the room (small, lack of furniture, repair needed etc.) was most often criticised by ERASMUS students going to France and Ireland

Table 6.8
Accommodation Problems Abroad (Principal Accommodation), by Host Country (percentage)

	Host Country											Total
	B	D	DK	E	F	GR	I	IRL	NL	P	UK	
Too small	33	21	9	27	34	26	24	20	23	32	30	29
Incomplete/inconvenient furniture or equipment	18	13	13	32	35	26	28	33	29	22	25	27
Problems of damp rooms, vermin, subst. repair needed	17	6	0	16	18	12	10	31	12	20	16	15
Sharing room with other students	9	9	13	15	11	26	41	13	15	44	5	12
Lack of privacy	10	14	6	22	19	37	30	17	23	32	14	18
Problems in sharing joint facilities with others	30	18	6	14	32	28	21	13	15	24	27	24
Noise or rude treatment by neighbours etc.	23	16	6	20	26	21	17	6	15	24	30	23
Restrictive regulations (visitors etc.)	13	8	6	7	18	5	25	10	3	2	7	11
Problems with owner/ manager/caretaker	7	11	13	9	10	14	17	5	6	12	5	9
Problems of security	12	6	6	5	22	16	5	6	7	0	9	11
Inconveniently located as regards host university	16	9	34	17	20	14	21	13	16	27	13	16
Inconveniently located as regards access to shops etc.	13	12	6	9	23	16	14	8	9	17	12	15
Other	7	6	6	10	11	9	15	14	9	7	9	10
Not ticked	19	34	41	21	13	14	16	26	29	15	21	21
Total	227	183	166	222	292	263	285	214	213	278	224	241
(n)	(94)	(371)	(32)	(314)	(849)	(43)	(210)	(109)	(188)	(41)	(961)	(3212)

Question 5.12: Which of the following problems did you experience (multiple reply possible)?

- disturbance by others (lack of privacy, problems of sharing rooms and facilities, problems with neighbours. etc.) was referred to most often by students who spent their period abroad in Portugal, Greece and Italy
- restrictive regulations, for example lack of rights to invite visitors to one's room, were most often reported by ERASMUS students going to Italy (25 %) and France (18 %)
- problems of security were most often stated by students who spent the study period in France (22 %). Such problems were also faced by a considerable proportion of students going to Greece (16 %).

University accommodation was not rated more favourably (2.7) than other kinds of accommodation in the host country (2.6). In the case of university accommodation, small size of room, problems of sharing facilities with others and or rude treatment by neighbours etc. were mentioned more often, whereas furniture and equipment problems were stated more often in the case of other kinds of accommodation.

Only seven percent of foreign students in the United Kingdom rated the quality of their accommodation as "bad" or "very bad"[4]. The respective proportions were 22 percent of all ERASMUS students and also 22 percent of ERASMUS students going to the United Kingdom. Asked about individual problems, more than 40 percent of foreign students in Britain complained about noise from neighbours and other tenants, 27 percent felt unsafe, and 14 percent reported problems with damp, vermin etc. (Hughes, 1990, pp. 54-5). Whereas ERASMUS students complained less about noise and safety risks, they more often considered their rooms as too small and inconveniently furnished. It seems appropriate to conclude that ERASMUS students on average had higher expectations regarding accommodation than foreign students in the United Kingdom, most of whom were more likely to complain if the most essential quality of accommodation was lacking.

The commuting time between university and the place where students lived was undoubtedly an important element in judging the quality of accommodation. Almost a third of the students spent more than half an hour on their daily return journey to the host university, eight percent of which spending even more than one hour. As only 16 percent

---

[4]   Hughes, 1990, p. 143.

had rated their accommodation as inconveniently located as regards the host university, the threshold of problematic location was on average a return journey lasting more than 50 minutes. This was reported:
- most often by students spending their period of study abroad in Spain (35 %) and Portugal (32 %), students spending some period in these countries spent on average 46 minutes
- somewhat above the mean by students going to Denmark (26 %) and Italy (22 %), guest students in both countries spent on average 36 minutes
- somewhat below the mean (11-15 %) by students going to the remaining countries, where students spent on average 25-32 minutes.

Therefore, students spent on average 30 minutes daily for the return journey to the university with about 45 minutes needed in Spain and Portugal.

The time needed to reach the university from university accommodation was usually shorter. 42 percent of students who lived in university accommodation spent up to only ten minutes for the daily return walk or trip to the university, a further 33 percent up to half an hour, and only 13 percent more than 50 minutes. On the other hand, only 19 percent of the other students lived so close to the university that they needed at most 10 minutes for both the way to the university and back to accommodation. A further 41 percent needed up to half an hour, whereas 22 percent had to spend more than 50 minutes. As the proportion of students living in halls of residence etc. while studying abroad was much higher than during the study period at home, we certainly can assume that the time spent for the return journey was on average less during the study period abroad than while studying at home.

6.6   Impact of Accommodation on Contacts

Accommodation abroad might be of help in getting informed about the host country and might provide opportunities for communication with host country people. Therefore, students were asked to state on a scale from 1 = "frequent" to 5 = "not at all" how frequently they had communication regarding various aspects with host country students or other host country people living in the same accommodation.

As Table 6.9 shows, communication with fellow residents was the most frequent means of acquiring knowledge regarding host country culture and society (60 % of the students rated 1 or 2). Also, support and advice regarding practical matters (52 %) as well as joint social activities (48 %) played a role. Discussions on academic matters were mentioned slightly less frequently (44 %). Finally, joint visits and travel were, as one might expect, reported less often, but still were not an infrequent experience (32 %).

In addition, students were asked to state the extent to which their accommodation was instrumental in establishing contacts with other people (on a scale from 1 = "very much" to 5 = "not at all"). In fact, many ERASMUS students reported that accommodation played an important role in establishing contacts with host country students (53 % rated 1 and 2) and - to the same extent - to students and other people from other countries (56 %). ERASMUS students reported less often that accommodation helped establish contacts with other host country people (29 %).

In comparing the responses to both questions by host country, we note that - across the various issues and activities - accommodation in Spain, the Federal Republic of Germany, Ireland and the United Kingdom was on average most supportive for increasing communication in the host country. In the case of Germany and the United Kingdom, ERASMUS students considered accommodation instrumental in establishing contact with students, whereas in the case of Ireland and Spain, ERASMUS students' accommodation strongly helped establish contact with other host country people.

As previous research has shown, university accommodation turns out to be very helpful in establishing contacts with students, but is of less help than other types of accommodation in establishing contacts with other host country people (see Chart 6.2). Thus, accommodation policies regarding foreign students also set the framework for the kind of social contacts most likely to develop.

Table 6.9
Role of Accommodation in Establishing Contacts (percent by host country)*

	Host Country											Total
	B	D	DK	E	F	GR	I	IRL	NL	P	UK	(n)
With host country students	46	70	59	51	42	40	50	45	42	41	62	53
With other host country people	27	28	28	54	22	30	26	59	23	37	27	29
With students/other people from other countries	52	65	32	41	56	36	46	42	46	32	65	56
Inform./discuss./coop. regarding academic matters	36	53	20	51	37	49	39	47	36	41	50	44
Information/discussion on culture, society etc.	51	67	50	69	50	57	53	71	57	56	66	60
Support and advice in practical matters	40	64	48	63	49	49	46	70	53	53	54	52
Joint social activities	37	51	31	56	42	49	52	48	38	33	54	48
Joint visits/travel	23	33	14	41	29	31	38	33	24	28	34	32

* Percent 1+2 on a scale from 1 = "very much" to 5 = " not at all"

Question 5.13: Was your accommodation instrumental in establishing contacts with other people? Question 5.14: What kind of interaction/communication did you have with host country students or other host country people living in the same accommodation?

Chart 6.2
Role of Accommodation in Establishing Contacts, by Type of Accommodation
(mean)

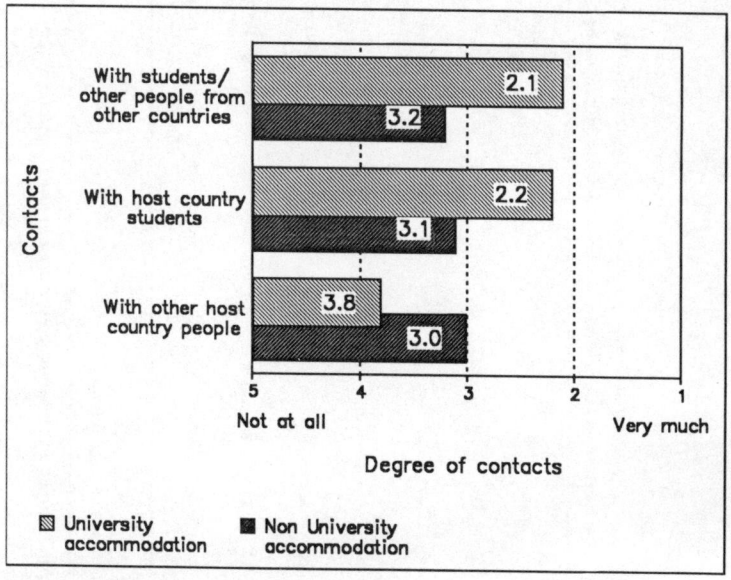

6.7 Suggestions for Improvement

Finally, students were asked to state who ought to be in charge of the search for accommodation and what social setting of accommodation they preferred. Students could choose from a scale from 1 = "strongly agree" to 5 = "strongly disagree" for each category provided (see Table 6.10).

As regards the social context of accommodation:

- 80 percent of the students agreed to the statement that the host university should arrange accommodation for guest students
- 48 percent supported the view that special university housing should be allocated predominantly to ERASMUS students
- lesser support (27 %) was voiced for the solution that most students should live with host country families.

Table 6.10
Views Regarding Accommodation of ERASMUS Students by Country of Home University (percentage)*

	B	D	DK	E	F	GR	I	IRL	NL	P	UK	Total
				Country of home university								
Help from former ERASMUS grantees in finding accomm.	48	50	43	50	60	63	38	56	32	40	42	49
Provision of accomm. by former ERASMUS grantees	9	12	7	8	8	34	6	10	8	10	10	9
Allocation of special university housing	60	38	50	88	37	65	58	40	70	70	38	48
ERASMUS students should live with host count. families	32	33	25	26	30	17	30	21	12	10	22	27
ERASMUS students should live in univ. housings	71	78	91	78	80	68	84	87	77	50	82	80
Responsibility of host univ. for accommodation of all	79	68	86	86	87	92	83	95	82	90	80	80
ERASMUS students own search for accommodation	20	25	14	13	18	3	13	20	16	20	14	18

Question 5.15: How would you describe your view as regards to the following statements?

* Percent 1+2 on a scale from 1 = "strongly agree" to 5 = "strongly disagree"

Views in this respect varied more strongly according to country of home university than according to host country. Notably, Danish and Irish students were most strongly in favour of living in university housing among host country students. Spanish and Portuguese students most strongly supported the idea of having special university housing predominantly for university students while Dutch students were least in favour of living with host country families.

The solutions favoured were to some extent linked to the students' own experiences. For example, 42 percent of the students who lived abroad in a room in a family home favoured this compared with 26 percent who had not lived in a family. 86 percent of students who had lived abroad in university accommodation favoured ERASMUS students living in university houses among host country students compared with 72 percent who had not lived in university accommodation.

As regards the search for accommodation, most ERASMUS students (80 %) expected the host university to arrange accommodation for all students. Only 18 percent held the view that ERASMUS students should search for accommodation themselves. Students going to Ireland and to Spain most often expected students to search for themselves - i.e. students who had gone to host countries in which accommodation was actually least often sought by the host university and in which students least often lived in university halls of residence.

As regards home country, we note that German students least often expect the host university to arrange accommodation. This is not related to the kind of support experienced abroad but rather that German students generally seemed to expect less support on the part of the university for tasks outside the academic domain.

The role the students suggested partner universities should take in the search for accommodation did not correlate significantly with the experience of the students regarding their institutions' support in providing or searching for accommodation. This allows us to assume that many students do not consider the extent and kind of support they had in their search for accommodation as desirable.

About half of the ERASMUS students (49 %) agreed to the statement that ERASMUS students should, upon return, help students from partner universities in finding accommodation. A very small number (9 %), though, suggested that ERASMUS grantholders should be obliged to provide accommodation for one exchange student. This view varied more according to home than to host country. Notably, Greek students (34 %) were in favour of mutual provisions of rooms among exchange students.

Twelve percent of the students reported that they had made their room available to an exchange student while they were abroad with this phenomenon not systematically linked to the duration of the study abroad period. Dutch students (21 %) most often made their rooms available to exchange students, as Chart 6.3 shows.

Chart 6.3
Home Students' Assistance for Host Students in Search for Accommodation by Country of Home University (percentage)

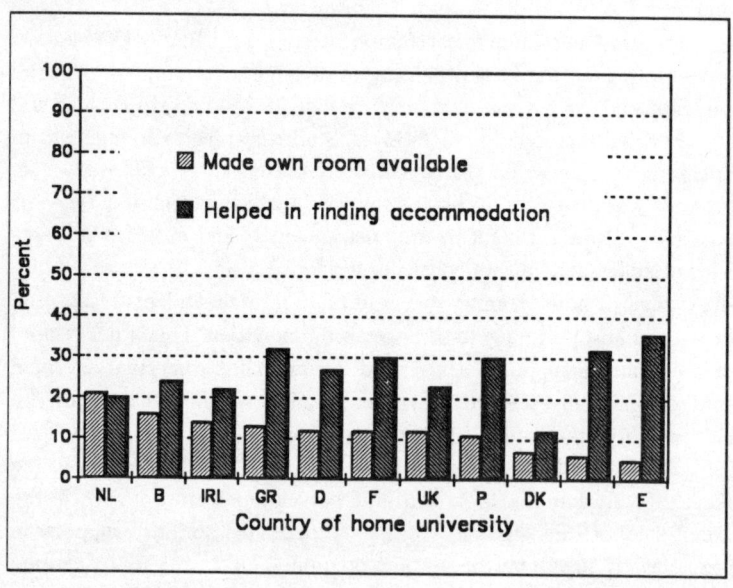

About 27 percent of the students reported that they helped students from partner institutions in finding accommodation - a surprisingly high figure, because only 14 percent of the students surveyed reported that they themselves were helped by students from the host institutions in finding accommodation, and only eight percent stated that host students were instrumental in providing accommodation. These discrepancies suggest that students only in part perceived that students at the partner university helped in finding accommodation.

Only 1.5 percent of the students surveyed seem to have reciprocally exchanged rooms. 14 percent of the students who had made available their room at home to an exchange student while they were abroad reported that they were provided regular accommodation by the host country students.

In general, there was a certain reciprocity of support regarding accommodation among the ERASMUS students. Whereas 27 percent of those students who did not experience help from students at the host university in finding accommodation, helped students from the host university in providing or finding accommodation, the amount of support was 55 percent when the students experienced help by students from the partner university.

Chapter 7

Costs and Financing of the Study Period Abroad

7.1 Monthly Expenses Abroad and at Home

The subsequent text and tables are based only on the responses of students who provided complete information on sources and expenses both while studying abroad and at home. This was done by 60 percent of all respondents.

On average, ERASMUS students spent about 419 ECU per month during the study period abroad in 1988/89. This sum did not include tuition and fees or the roundtrip fare to the host country. As Table 7.1 shows, the monthly average expenses varied substantially by host country. Those going to Denmark spent 506 ECU on average, and those going to the United Kingdom, Ireland, Italy and Spain about 450 ECU. Those going to Greece spent about 400 ECU, those going to France, the Netherlands, Belgium and Germany somewhat less, and those going to Portugal only 331 ECU.

The differences found by host country consistently did not match assumptions about differences in general living expenses. There were various factors which might lead to unexpectedly high expenditures, for example shortage of reasonable accommodation, relatively short study periods which might lead to higher costs per month, students' difficulties in adjusting to food and the lifestyle prevailing in the host country. On the other hand, general subsidies to studies, food, accommodation etc. in some countries served the hosts students well and thus reduced the costs of living abroad.

The monthly expenses abroad varied less by duration of the study period at the host institution than one might have expected. As Chart 7.1 shows, those going abroad for three months spent 435 ECU per month on average (excluding return travel to the host institution), those going abroad for 4-6 months 423 ECU and those going abroad for 7-12 months 398 ECU. It might be added that those only going abroad for less than three months reported expenses of 370 ECU, whereas those staying abroad longer than one year reported higher expenses (480 ECU).

While studying at home, ERASMUS students had spent 355 ECU monthly on average. As indicated by Table 7.2, Danish students reported the highest expenses per month while studying at home (472 ECU), while German, British, Italian and Dutch students spent almost 400 ECU, and French, Spanish and Belgian students somewhat more than 300 ECU. Finally, Irish, Greek and Portuguese students spent less than 300 ECU while studying at home.

Thus, the monthly expenses abroad - excluding roundtrip fare, tuition and fees - were 64 ECU (18.0 %) higher than expenses at home. Table 7.3 shows the expenses borne abroad by students of the various home countries. As indicated in the first column of Table 7.4, the additional costs abroad thus calculated varied strikingly according to home country.

On average, the roundtrip travel costs to the host country added 30 ECU to the monthly expenses abroad. They varied from 75 ECU among those going to Portugal and Greece, to just over 20 ECU for students going to France and Germany. Both the peripheral location of the former countries within Europe and the relatively short average duration of the study period abroad among students going there explain the high monthly roundtrip travel costs.

On average, monthly expenses abroad including roundtrip travel amounted to 449 ECU (not including additional costs for tuition and fees) - 94 ECU (26 %) higher than expenses at home. Respective differences according to home country are presented in the third column of Table 7.4.

Table 7.1
Monthly Expenditures During the Study Period Abroad*, by Host Country (in ECU, mean)

	Host country												Total
	B	D	DK	E	F	GR	I	IRL	NL	P	UK	
Books and other study-related supplies	27.1	20.5	25.9	26.4	21.5	28.9	25.1	25.0	29.6	18.7	30.8	25.8
Accommodation	107.5	115.3	184.3	154.7	124.0	132.6	148.0	152.9	132.0	97.0	171.1	143.4
Travel to university	9.3	16.3	16.1	14.1	16.6	11.7	16.5	15.1	17.2	22.3	14.5	15.4
Other travel	35.7	32.2	66.5	43.2	40.2	66.0	51.0	48.1	37.6	21.9	44.6	42.0
Food, common household clothes, hygiene etc.	178.0	157.2	180.0	175.8	164.1	151.6	173.4	183.9	135.2	144.3	172.0	166.5
Other expenses	20.7	17.0	33.6	28.5	24.6	18.5	31.5	25.2	35.4	26.7	26.2	25.7
Total	378.3	358.4	506.3	442.6	391.0	404.3	445.4	450.3	387.1	330.9	459.2	419.1
Return travel abroad	34.2	22.9	43.9	32.9	21.5	74.1	37.6	40.0	29.7	74.9	29.8	29.2
(n)	(65)	(214)	(26)	(195)	(482)	(23)	(130)	(70)	(115)	(27)	(575)	(1922)

Question 2.9: Apart from tuition fees and related expenses: How much, on average, did you spend per month during term time during your study period abroad and while studying at home? Please state the amount in the currency of the country of your home university.

* Excluding tuition and fees and excluding return travel

Table 7.2
Monthly Expenditures While Studying at Home*, by Country of Home University (in ECU, mean)

	Country of home university											Total
	B	D	DK	E	F	GR	I	IRL	NL	P	UK	
Books and other study-related supplies	34.3	32.7	46.2	40.9	19.4	31.2	37.4	18.7	31.9	20.0	28.3	29.8
Accommodation	93.8	115.6	160.7	82.0	114.3	53.2	98.6	73.2	121.6	34.4	171.7	123.2
Travel to university	22.2	18.1	11.4	17.6	20.3	13.0	20.3	13.1	16.5	12.5	21.7	19.4
Other travel	14.5	33.3	25.3	26.4	20.1	23.1	29.6	19.5	19.8	4.8	21.8	24.7
Food, common household, clothes, hygiene etc.	122.5	156.7	210.0	127.3	133.8	111.6	170.0	109.4	156.4	43.1	116.0	138.6
Other expenses	13.8	21.4	18.8	19.2	18.7	29.1	20.8	12.2	22.2	.0	19.2	19.6
Total	301.1	377.9	472.4	313.5	326.8	261.2	376.8	246.1	368.4	114.8	378.6	355.3

Question 2.9: Apart from tuition fees and related expenses: How much, on average, did you spend per month during term time during your study period abroad and while studying at home? Please state the amount in the currency of the country of your home university.

* Excluding tuition and fees

Table 7.3
Monthly Expenditures During the Study Period Abroad*, by Country of Home University (in ECU, mean)

	B	D	DK	E	F	GR	I	IRL	NL	P	UK	Total
Books and other study-related supplies	26.6	32.2	49.6	37.3	21.0	42.6	27.8	21.1	23.0	26.0	16.8	25.8
Accommodation	143.6	151.7	181.6	140.4	152.3	152.6	158.1	122.7	122.8	109.2	125.9	143.4
Travel to university	22.1	14.1	20.6	11.3	14.4	10.7	21.9	18.7	11.8	2.9	16.2	15.4
Return travel abroad	26.5	25.4	43.3	26.9	25.3	62.3	37.4	35.1	30.4	59.2	33.9	29.7
Other travel	22.6	55.9	70.1	54.7	22.8	56.7	40.8	36.1	29.6	9.0	45.8	42.0
Food, common household, clothes, hygiene etc.	148.7	186.8	238.3	161.1	157.0	221.0	190.2	147.3	197.7	70.0	138.0	166.7
Other expenses	19.0	28.2	38.5	19.9	19.4	42.8	23.3	15.1	32.2	.0	29.8	25.7
Total - abroad	409.0	494.3	641.9	451.6	412.2	588.7	499.6	396.0	447.5	276.3	406.3	448.8

Question 2.9: Apart from tuition fees and related expenses: How much, on average, did you spend per month during term time during your study period abroad and while studying at home? Please state the amount in the currency of the country of your home university.

* Excluding tuition and fees

Chart 7.1
**Monthly Expenditures - Excluding Return Travel Abroad - by Duration of Study
Period Abroad** (in ECU, mean)

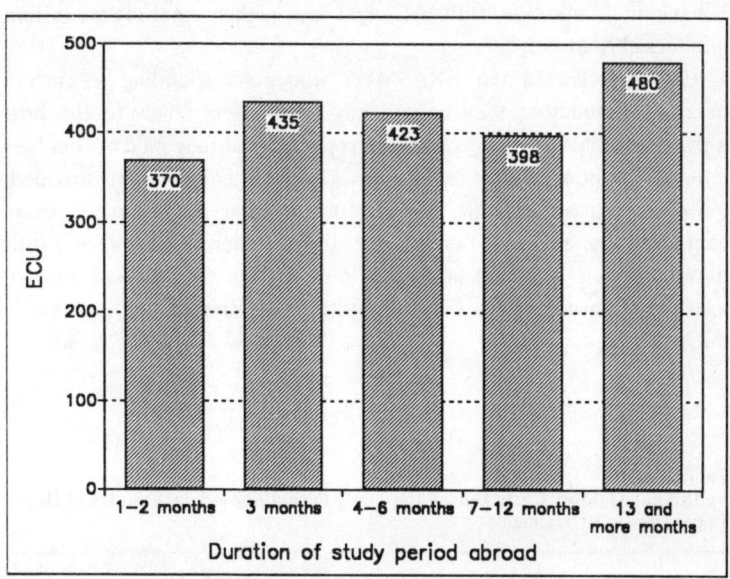

If this estimate is correct, monthly expenses abroad - excluding
roundtrip fare to the host country - were on average 105 ECU (29 %)
higher than monthly costs at home. The differences according to home
country are presented in column 2 of Table 7.4. Including roundtrip fare
to the host country, the average monthly expenses abroad (thus
estimated) surpassed those at home by 135 ECU (37 %). As the fourth
column of Table 7.4 shows, we estimate that:
- Greek students had more than 300 ECU additional monthly expenses
  during the study period abroad
- Danish students more than 200 ECU
- Irish, Portuguese, Spanish, Italian and German students more than
  150 ECU
- Belgian, French and Dutch students had less than 150 ECU
  additional expenses
- British students only 80 ECU additional monthly expenses abroad.

One should bear in mind that this data neither show price differences nor indicate needs for financial means as such, but rather actual behaviour. In addition, students might face higher expenses for tuition and fees abroad.

Eight percent of the ERASMUS students responding to such a question stated that they had to pay tuition fees solely at the host university while a further six percent reported that they paid tuition fees both at the home and the host university. The information provided, however, was not reliable, because it was clear that many students confused other fees (for example for student union or insurances) with tuition fees or recorded additional fees for the total period abroad, instead of on a monthly basis. Despite these caveats, we estimate it might be appropriate to add about a further 10 ECU per month on average.

Table 7.4
Additional Monthly Costs During the Study Period Abroad, by Country of Home University (in ECU, mean)

Country of home university	Excluding roundtrip travel		Including roundtrip travel	
	Additional costs stated	Additional costs including continued costs at home*	Additional costs stated	Additional costs including continued costs at home*
Greece	265	283	328	346
Denmark	126	180	170	224
Ireland	115	139	150	174
Portugal	102	113	161	172
Spain	111	138	138	165
Italy	85	118	129	156
Germany	91	130	116	155
Belgium	81	112	108	139
France	60	98	85	123
Netherlands	49	90	79	120
United Kingdom	-6	51	28	85
Total ECU	64	105	94	135

* Estimate based on the assumption that a third of the ERASMUS students keep their accommodation in the country of the home institution while studying abroad.

So far, we have addressed average expenses only. It is necessary, however, to take into account the frequencies as well. Looking at the differences between living expenses abroad and at home (excluding roundtrip fare to the host country), as defined in the first column of Table 7.4, we note that 16 percent of the ERASMUS students had at least ten percent less expenses abroad than while studying at home, 18 percent had about the same expenses abroad they had at home (between 10 % less and 10 % more) while 35 percent of students had between ten and 50 percent additional costs abroad. Finally, 31 percent had more than 50 percent additional costs abroad.

In adding the estimated costs for keeping accommodation in the country of the home institution while studying abroad (excluding roundtrip fare to the host country and excluding additional costs for tuition and fees) we estimate that:

- 9 percent of the ERASMUS students had at least ten percent less expenses abroad than during a corresponding period at home
- 14 percent had about the same expenses abroad they had at home
- 36 percent had ten to 50 percent higher costs abroad
- 41 percent had more than 50 percent additional costs abroad.

7.2   Resources for Funding Study Abroad and at Home

Almost all students provided information about their resources of financing the study period at the host institution. As Table 7.5 shows, about 42 percent of the expenses of their study period abroad were financed by the students themselves or their families, 35 percent by the ERASMUS grant and 19 percent by other grants and loans. The ERASMUS grant covered about half of the expenses for Portuguese, Italian, Greek, Belgian and Spanish students, about a third for German and Irish students and slightly more than a quarter for French, Danish and British students. French students had to cover the highest proportion of the ERASMUS supported period by help of their families and by their own means (53 %), followed by German and Greek students (47 % each). On the other hand, Danish (8 %), Portuguese (13 %) and Dutch students (20 %) reported the lowest private contribution to the ERASMUS supported period abroad, because of home country fellowships covering a high proportion of their expenses 'abroad (39, 33 and 41 % respectively).

Table 7.5
Financing of Study Period Abroad, by Country of Home University (percentage)

	Country of home university											Total
	B	D	DK	E	F	GR	I	IRL	NL	P	UK	
ERASMUS grant	51.2	36.3	25.4	50.1	28.5	49.3	54.3	34.4	28.5	55.0	27.6	35.2
Other European Comm-unity programme grant	.0	.1	.0	.0	.0	.0	.0	.0	.0	.0	.2	.1
Home country grant/scholarship	2.2	1.7	38.8	6.3	7.8	1.7	1.9	16.6	40.9	32.5	29.6	13.0
Home country loan	.2	10.3	15.1	1.0	3.2	.0	.0	7.9	5.9	.0	1.4	4.5
Host country grant/scholarship	.7	.1	4.6	.4	.5	.0	.0	.0	.0	.0	.6	.4
Support by work placement or employer	.3	1.2	.3	.0	2.2	.0	.0	3.7	.0	.0	3.2	1.6
Other type of support abroad	.8	.4	.0	.4	.4	.0	.5	1.5	.3	.0	.2	.4
Other grants	.0	.2	7.7	1.1	1.8	2.4	.8	2.7	1.1	.0	.9	1.0
Parents, relatives	36.9	32.5	1.7	30.1	42.6	35.2	33.6	12.5	11.3	7.5	27.9	31.6
Own money (work, savings)	6.6	14.5	6.7	10.4	10.6	11.3	7.9	20.7	9.6	5.0	7.0	10.4
Other	.4	1.0	1.8	.2	1.7	.0	.3	.0	2.0	.0	.5	1.0
Total	100.0	100.0	100.0	100.0	100.0	100.0	100.0	100.0	100.0	100.0	100.0	100.0
(n)	(124)	(514)	(36)	(122)	(392)	(29)	(116)	(31)	(108)	(4)	(446)	(1922)

Question 2.7: How have you financed your study at your home university up to now, and how did you finance your ERASMUS-supported study period abroad (including travel and tuition fees if any)? Please estimate percentages (including possibly value of free rent, etc.). If applicable, state the name of the support scheme or of the supporting agency.

Table 7.6
Financing of Study at Home University, by Country of Home University (percentage)

	Country of home university											Total
	B	D	DK	E	F	GR	I	IRL	NL	P	UK	
Other European Community programme grant	.0	.3	.0	.0	.1	1.7	.0	1.3	.5	.0	.0	.2
Home country grant/scholarship	8.4	1.5	52.5	21.8	13.4	7.2	4.7	39.2	60.7	5.0	45.8	21.1
Home country loan	.7	15.6	18.4	1.1	3.0	.0	.0	4.5	9.8	.0	1.8	6.3
Support by work placement or employer	.0	.8	1.1	.1	.8	.7	.0	3.2	.7	.0	1.4	.8
Other grants	.1	.4	.3	1.1	.9	.3	1.7	2.6	.5	.0	1.1	.8
Parents, relatives	81.6	58.4	4.1	65.0	67.9	76.2	82.4	24.6	15.7	87.5	41.0	56.0
Own money (work, savings)	8.4	21.2	23.6	10.0	11.6	13.1	10.2	23.6	10.5	7.5	7.1	13.1
Other	.3	1.5	.0	.9	2.0	.7	.3	1.1	.9	.0	1.0	1.2
Total	100.0	100.0	100.0	100.0	100.0	100.0	100.0	100.0	100.0	100.0	100.0	100.0
(n)	(124)	(514)	(36)	(122)	(392)	(29)	(116)	(31)	(108)	(4)	(446)	(1922)

Question 2.7: How have you financed your study at your home university up to now, and how did you finance your ERASMUS-supported study period abroad (including travel and tuition fees if any)? Please estimate percentages (including possibly value of free rent, etc.). If applicable, state the name of the support scheme or of the supporting agency.

Table 7.6 shows that ERASMUS students and their parents have paid more than two thirds (69 %) of the expenses incurred while studying at the home institution. The corresponding proportion was 42 percent for the study period abroad, as already reported above. The information provided by the students suggests that parents and students themselves covered 246 ECU of the monthly expenses while the students were at the home university, and 188 ECU of the expenses abroad. The absolute amount of other grants and loans was more or less the same on average for the study period abroad as for study at the home institution.

In combining the replies to the questions on expenses abroad (absolute figures were asked for) and those on the financial sources (percentages were asked for), we estimate that the average monthly ERASMUS support was 158 ECU in 1988/89. This does not include ERASMUS support used for costs prior to the study abroad period (notably language courses). The monthly ERASMUS support, therefore, surpassed that of the average additional expenses abroad (including return travel to the host institution and including estimated costs for keeping accommodation at home) by 23 ECU on average. Even including estimated additional costs for tuition and fees, we conclude that the ERASMUS grants in 1988/89 on average covered the additional costs associated with study abroad.

Notably, Italian, Belgian and Spanish students on average reported higher ERASMUS grants than additional costs abroad. On the other hand, the ERASMUS grant did not cover the average additional costs in the cases of Greek, Danish and Irish students.

7.3   Financial Problems during the Study Period in the Host Country

As discussed in Chapter 5, students were provided with a list of 19 categories of possible problems during their stay abroad. On a scale from 1 = "very serious problems" to 5 = "no problems at all", financial problems were rated more seriously on average (3.5) than any other possible problem. In fact, 21 percent of the students reported "very serious" or "serious" financial problems. This proportion was by far the highest among Irish ERASMUS students (54 %), though serious problems were also stated relatively frequently by Greek (34 %), Portuguese (30 %), British (28 %) and French students (24 %). Least problems were reported by Danish students (2 %), while 15 - 21 percent of the students from the remaining countries stated financial problems.

Financial problems varied to a much lesser extent according to the host country. Those going to Italy (34 %), Spain (29 %) and Portugal (24 %) reported problems more frequently than those going to other countries.

19 percent of the students who had lived with their parents or relatives when studying in their home country, reported financial problems while studying abroad. Among those who had lived away from home when they studied in their home country, 22 percent reported financial problems abroad. This small difference corresponds with the previous finding, that students who lived with their parents or relatives before they went abroad had on average slightly more funds available abroad than those who lived somewhere else while studying in their home country.

In explaining the financial problems reported by Irish students we first note that Irish ERASMUS students spent very little while studying at home and studying abroad (only the Portuguese spend less; see Tables 7.2 and 7.3). Second, Irish students and their parents had to bear higher expenses per month for the study period abroad (about 131 ECU) than while studying at the home institution (about 119 ECU, including value of free rent, etc.), whereas the reverse is true for students from most other countries. This can only in part be explained by the fact that the monthly ERASMUS support to Irish students (about 196 ECU) is below average for all ERASMUS students in general - lower only for British (about 112 ECU), French (about 118 ECU) and Dutch students (about 128 ECU).

It should be noted that Irish students who lived with their parents or relatives before the ERASMUS supported period received on average substantially higher ERASMUS support than those who did not live with their parents or relatives. This higher ERASMUS support, however, did not make up for the additional expenses. Rather, the students living at home spent an additional 33 ECU monthly abroad not covered by the ERASMUS grant in comparison with 16 ECU for the students not living at home; in total the students living at home spent 31 ECU less per month abroad than the students not living at home. This data indicate that Irish students who lived with their parents and relatives while studying at home spent more of their parents' and their own means during the ERASMUS period while having to live, in spite of that, a more thrifty life abroad than other Irish ERASMUS students.

One would expect from this data that those Irish ERASMUS students who lived with their parents while studying in their home country were most likely to report financial problems during their study abroad period. Actually, however, "only" 42 percent of them reported serious financial problems compared with 59 percent of those Irish students who did not live with their parents and relatives while studying in their home country.

In the case of Greek students, we note that average expenses at home were the third lowest, while expenses abroad were the second highest. Even if we exclude the costs for the round trip fare to the host institution, Greek students spent 111 percent more abroad per month than they spent at home (compared with 18 percent among all ERASMUS supported students). In almost all categories (books and other materials, travelling in the host country, food and various household expenses as well as other expenses abroad), they belonged to those reporting the highest expenses. Although the monthly ERASMUS support for Greek students was the highest on average (about 290 ECU), Greek students and their parents bore higher expenses during the study abroad period (about 274 ECU) than while studying at home (233 ECU, since Greece belongs to those countries where a high proportion of ERASMUS students lived at home prior to the ERASMUS supported period abroad).

7.4   The Role Played by ERASMUS Support

Altogether, the information provided by the students suggests that the ERASMUS grant was slightly higher on average than all additional expenses abroad (including estimated continuous costs at home and additional costs for tuition and fees). The ERASMUS grant even seemed to cover on average the additional expenses for students who lived with their parents or relatives prior to the study period abroad.

This does not necessarily mean, however, that the ERASMUS grant solved all problems related to additional costs of a study period abroad. As shown above, some students received a smaller ERASMUS grant than additional costs which they actually incurred in the context of their study abroad period (while other students received a higher grant than costs incurred). In addition, the comparison made does not necessarily reveal all financial means and expenses; for example, students might have had opportunities of earning money while studying at home which did not exist while studying abroad. Further, information about the actual expenses did not reveal how many students might have been compelled to choose thriftier living conditions abroad; this was certainly the fact for many among the 21 percent of the ERASMUS students who reported financial problems. Finally, a survey on ERASMUS students by definition cannot reveal how many students did not apply for ERASMUS support or did not go abroad when offered ERASMUS support because they considered the financial support too small.

Chapter 8

Recognition and Academic Impacts

8.1 Need for Varied Measures of "Recognition"

Recognition of the ERASMUS supported period in another EC Member State upon return is one of the most crucial measures of success of the ERASMUS programme. In principle, ERASMUS support is only granted to departments and universities willing to recognize the academic achievements of their students upon return. This emphasis on recognition is based on the assumption that a study period in another country of the European Community will most likely become an integral part of studies, if successful study at a host university substitutes for study loads or study periods at home.

A survey conducted in the mid-eighties on a select number of Joint Study Programmes, i.e. programmes supported by the EC support scheme preceding the ERASMUS programme, had shown that complete recognition for all students was unlikely to be achieved. 79 percent of programme directors of a select number of relatively successful JSPs stated that the entire programme abroad was recognized as a rule, and 72 percent of the students reported that their entire study activities abroad were recognized upon return. In comparison, 81 percent of JSPs directors stated that participating students did not have to expect any prolongation of study due to the study period abroad, nor did 71 percent of the students participating in JSP, surveyed a few weeks after returning to their home university, expect any.[1]

---

[1]   U. Teichler and W. Steube. "The Logics of Study Abroad Programmes and Their Impacts", *Higher Education*, Vol., No. 3, 1991.

In the questionnaire survey of 1988/89 ERASMUS students, we chose three different measures of recognition:

(a) *degree of recognition*: the degree to which the academic study actually undertaken at the host university was recognized or otherwise considered equivalent to study at the home university
(b) *degree of correspondence*: the degree of correspondence of the amount of study abroad and study at home
(c) *non-prolongation*: the expected non-prolongation of the total duration of studies due to the study period at the host university.

The three different criteria were chosen because the definition of recognition might vary. First, students might take a reduced study load abroad; if this is fully recognized, study at the host university does not fully correspond to study at home. Second, there might be a gap between the degree of correspondence between the amount of study abroad and at home and the likelihood of avoiding prolongation due to study abroad. Some students might face prolongation, even if their studies were considered as fully corresponding to studies at home, and some students might avoid prolongation, even if their studies at the host universities were considered as not fully corresponding to the amount of study at their home university.

The percentages in the subsequent tables refer only to those students actually stating that recognition was granted or expected. Some students had not (yet) returned to the home university at the time the survey was conducted; in other cases, the recognition procedure was not yet completed. 69 percent of the students provided information on the degree of recognition, 64 percent estimated the degree of correspondence of study at the host university with that at the home university, and 87 percent replied to the questions regarding possible prolongation of studies due to study abroad.

8.2 Degree of Recognition

As Table 8.1 shows, 23 percent of the studies actually undertaken at the host universities were not recognised upon return. Credit was granted for about half of the studies at the host university. A third of the studies were otherwise considered equivalent. The latter category was needed, because studies abroad might be recognized in other ways, for example,

Table 8.1
Recognition of Study Abroad at Host University, by Country of Home University (percentage of amount and mean of types of recognition)

	Country of home university											Total
	B	D	DK	E	F	GR	I	IRL	NL	P	UK	
100% and more	78	61	82	51	84	56	68	83	72	80	58	68
75% - 99%	2	5	3	3	2	17	11	0	4	0	1	4
50% - 74%	8	8	11	8	4	6	11	0	11	0	7	7
25% - 49%	5	5	0	8	2	0	2	0	2	0	4	4
less than 25%	7	22	5	31	8	22	8	14	10	20	29	17
Total	100	100	100	100	100	100	100	100	100	100	100	100
(n)	(123)	(684)	(38)	(159)	(559)	(18)	(179)	(29)	(89)	(5)	(320)	(2203)
Credit granted	50.9	55.6	83.7	25.2	40.3	36.7	70.8	48.3	70.9	60.0	35.0	48.4
Otherwise considered equivalent	43.0	16.3	7.2	35.0	64.0	37.5	13.5	39.7	12.6	20.0	32.0	33.5
Neither credit granted nor otherwise considered equivalent	14.0	28.5	9.6	39.8	10.8	25.8	16.2	15.5	16.5	20.0	33.3	22.7

Question 4.9: To what extent is your academic study at the host university granted credit or otherwise considered equivalent to studies at the home university?

global recognition of the whole period, exams referring to whole periods, or more open arrangements in which only part of the courses abroad or at home had to be credited.

Actually, 68 percent of the students reported that all their study at the host university was recognized (or otherwise considered equivalent) upon return by the home university. On the other hand, 17 percent were credited for less than a quarter of their study at the host university.

8.3 Degree of Correspondence of Amount of Study

Table 8.2 presents the degree of correspondence of the amount of study at home and host universities for respective proportions of students.[2] Only 40 percent of the students reported that the amount of study abroad equalled that at home or even surpassed it, a further 41 percent had a study load abroad of at least half of that typical at home, and 19 percent less than half of that at home.

On average for all ERASMUS students responding, academic studies at the host university corresponded to 73 percent of the typical amount of study at the home university. As 77 percent of the studies abroad were recognized and as the study load actually taken abroad or the number of courses completed abroad was about one sixth lower than that typically carried out or completed during a corresponding period at home, one could have expected that the academic studies at the host university corresponded to a lesser extent to the typical amount of study at home.

---

2   In the questionnaire, students had been asked to state (a) the percentage of credits granted for the period abroad corresponding to credits typically granted or otherwise considered equivalent at their home university, and (b) the percentage of all academic study abroad corresponding to typical study at their home university. As the replies to (a) and (b) did not differ substantially and as some students replied only to one category, replies were merged in the subsequent Tables. If available, responses to (b) were chosen; responses to (a) are taken into account only if no information was supplied to (b).

Table 8.2
Correspondence of Academic Study Abroad to Typical Amount of Study at Home University, by Country of Home University (percentage)

	Country of home university											Total
	B	D	DK	E	F	GR	I	IRL	NL	P	UK	
100 %	47	43	62	46	28	50	30	69	52	50	41	40
75% - 99%	12	16	19	12	17	17	15	7	19	38	14	15
50% - 74%	19	27	17	21	32	25	37	10	6	13	21	26
25% - 49%	15	6	0	9	13	0	9	7	4	0	11	9
Less than 25%	9	8	2	12	10	8	8	7	18	0	13	10
Total	100	100	100	100	100	100	100	100	100	100	100	100
(n)	(129)	(661)	(42)	(164)	(498)	(24)	(214)	(29)	(113)	(8)	(375)	(2257)
Ratio of correspondence	72.7	76.4	96.9	72.8	65.3	81.9	71.3	84.5	82.4	100.0	71.6	73.1

Question 4.10: To what extent does your study at the host university actually correspond to the amount of typical study at the home university during a corresponding period?

8.4   Non-Prolongation of Study due to Study Period Abroad

On average, ERASMUS students expected 3.4 months prolongation due to their study period abroad. The prolongation expected corresponds to 53 percent of the study period abroad (the figures refer to students providing information both on prolongation and duration of the period abroad). As Table 8.3 shows, the ratio of prolongation did not vary substantially according to the duration of the study period. Only in cases where students went abroad with the help of the ERASMUS programme for more than one year were study periods abroad so closely integrated into the curriculum that very few students expected a prolongation due to the study periods abroad.

56 percent of the students did not expect a prolongation of their studies. 12 percent assumed that there would be a prolongation due to study abroad, though shorter than the period they had spent abroad. 33 percent of the students, however, stated that the prolongation of studies due to study abroad would be as long as the study period abroad (in a few cases even more).

Table 8.3
**Ratio of Prolongation of Study and Duration of Study Period Abroad, by
Duration** (percentage)

	Duration of study abroad					Total
	1-2 months	3 months	4-6 months	7-12 months	More than 12 months	
None	79	67	56	41	85	56
Less than 50 %	0	3	3	5	3	4
50% - 74%	3	3	5	9	11	6
75% - 99%	0	0	3	3	1	2
100%	18	27	34	42	1	33
Total	100	100	100	100	100	100
(n)	(76)	(594)	(986)	(962)	(157)	(2775)
Ratio of prolongation	58.6	52.9	53.0	59.9	8.3	53.0

Question 4.11: The study period abroad is likely to prolong the total duration of my study by:

8.5 Comparison and Interrelationships between Criteria of Recognition

Thus, the extent of recognition of study abroad was 77 percent on average if we address the "degree of recognition" of what was studied abroad, and 73 percent on average if the amount of study abroad was compared to that usually taken at home. It involved only 47 percent recognition if we take the students' expectation as a yardstick for studies at the host university not leading to prolongation of the total duration of study (see Chart 8.1). A considerable number of students had to face a prolongation of their studies at the home university by more than 100 percent of the period they spent abroad, e.g. due to the different timing of academic terms in the Member States.

The proportion of students who reported full recognition was smaller. It was 68 percent, if we refer to ERASMUS students who reported that all academic studies at the host university were granted credit or otherwise considered equivalent; 40 percent, if we take into account students stating that all academic study at the host university corresponded to 100 percent (or even more) of typical study at the home university; and

56 percent, if we take the students expecting no prolongation of study due to their study period abroad.

Chart 8.1
Recognition According to Different Criteria, all Students (percentage)

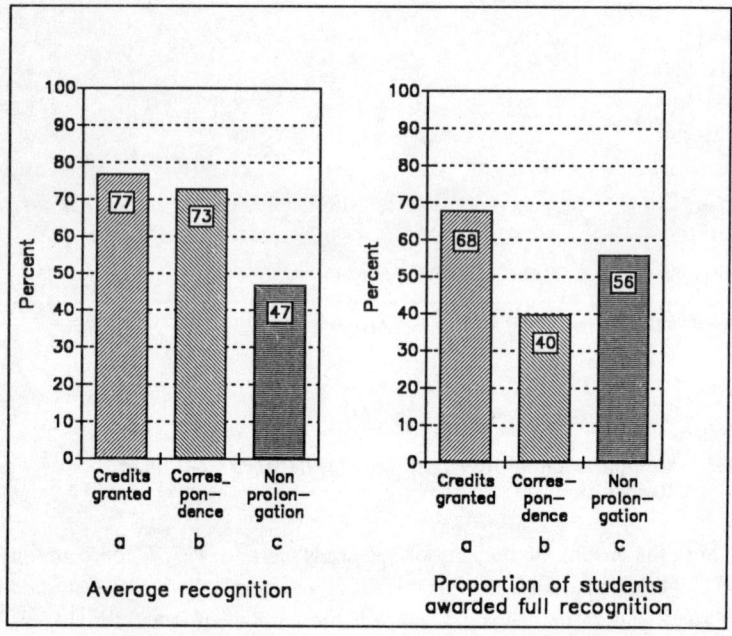

The proportion of ERASMUS students who experienced full recognition was lower than that of students supported by the JSP scheme who were surveyed in the mid-eighties: the respective figures are 68 and 72 percent for the first measure, and 56 and 71 percent for the third measure (Teichler and Steube, 1991). A lower ratio of recognition for ERASMUS students was not surprising, because many Inter-University Cooperation Programmes supported by ERASMUS had existed only for a short period at the time this survey was conducted, whereas the JSP programmes included in the survey conducted in the mid-eighties had existed for some years at that time. Also, we cannot exclude the possibility that a high degree of recognition would be more easily achieved if the scale of study abroad programmes was not as large as it became with the inauguration of the ERASMUS programme. Surveys on future cohorts of ERASMUS students might provide more convincing explanations.

In analysing the relationships between the degree of recognition and degree of correspondence, we note that 45 percent of the students reported the quota for both while 40 percent reported a lower degree of correspondence than that of recognition. On the other hand, 15 percent of students received (full or partial) recognition abroad with less amount of work involved than would be usual at home.

In addressing the relationships between the degree of recognition and the degree of non-prolongation we observe that at least a quarter of the ERASMUS students reported a higher percentage of prolongation of studies when the percentage of studies abroad was not recognized or otherwise considered equivalent. On the other hand, about one eighth of the students expected less prolongation of study than one could have predicted on the basis of information of study abroad not recognized or otherwise considered equivalent upon return.

Finally, we analysed the links between responses regarding the degree of correspondence and non-prolongation. 34 percent faced prolongation, which should be less or not faced at all if the non-correspondence between the amount of study abroad and home clearly determined prolongation. Of those whose amount of study abroad equalled that typically expected at home, 66 percent expected no pro-longation, 13 percent some prolongation, and 21 percent a prolongation as long as the study period abroad. 28 percent of the students faced lesser prolongation than one could have expected from their infor-mation about the amount of study abroad (or even no prolongation in spite of a lesser amount of study abroad than typically expected at home).

8.6 Self-Rating of Academic Progress Abroad

ERASMUS students in 1988/89 rated their academic progress during the period at the host university quite positively. Asked to compare the progress abroad with what they would have expected in a corresponding period at home, they rated it 2.5 on average on a scale from 1 = "much better" to 5 = "much less". They rated their academic progress abroad more positively on average than participants of "Joint Study Programmes" surveyed in the mid-eighties (2.8).

55 percent of the ERASMUS students actually rated their academic progress at the host university more positively than academic progress at home, and 26 percent stated that it was on the same level. Only 19 percent considered the progress abroad to be lower than at home, as Table 8.4 shows.

Table 8.4
Academic Progress Abroad in Comparison to Study at Home University, by Country of Home University (percentage and mean)

	Country of home university											Total
	B	D	DK	E	F	GR	I	IRL	NL	P	UK	
1 = Much better	23	15	14	33	31	51	24	10	15	10	16	22
2	35	30	25	33	35	30	45	30	31	50	29	33
3 = Same	33	28	20	19	22	14	17	35	35	40	28	26
4	7	20	36	13	9	5	11	20	15	0	21	15
5 = Much less	2	6	5	1	3	0	3	5	4	0	7	4
Total	100	100	100	100	100	100	100	100	100	100	100	100
(n)	(213)	(782)	(44)	(301)	(658)	(37)	(282)	(40)	(151)	(10)	(618)	(3136)
Academic Progress abroad	2.3	2.7	2.9	2.2	2.2	1.7	2.2	2.8	2.6	2.3	2.7	2.5

Question 6.4: How would you rate your general academic progress during your study period abroad, compared with what you would have expected in a corresponding period at your home university?

The rating of academic progress abroad did not significantly differ according to the duration of the study period abroad. It differed somewhat by the timing of the study period abroad: students who had studied three years or more at home before they went abroad assessed the academic progress abroad more positively than those going abroad at an earlier stage of their studies. This, however, might be due to home and host country effects.

The assessment of academic progress abroad varied more according to home country than according to host country, as a comparison between Table 8.4 and Table 8.5 shows. Expectations derived from and conditions of the home university seemed to affect the self-rating of achievement abroad more strongly than the specific experiences and conditions at the host universities.

Table 8.5
Academic Progress Abroad, by Host Country (percentage and mean)

	B	D	DK	E	F	GR	I	IRL	NL	P	UK	Total
					Host country							Total
1 = Much better	20	24	38	21	19	9	19	18	22	15	26	22
2	35	36	44	34	32	33	31	24	34	26	33	33
3 = Same	33	25*	16	24	26	40	26	33	28	36	23	26
4	9	12	3	14	18	14	16	20	11	23	15	15
5 = Much less	4	4	0	6	5	5	9	6	5	0	2	4
Total	100	100	100	100	100	100	100	100	100	100	100	100
(n)	(92)	(363)	(32)	(304)	(820)	(43)	(206)	(106)	(186)	(39)	(945)	(3136)
Academic progress abroad	2.4	2.4	1.8	2.5	2.6	2.7	2.6	2.7	2.4	2.7	2.3	2.5

Question 6.4: How would you rate your general academic progress during your study period abroad, compared with what you would have expected in a corresponding period at your home university?

Altogether we note that students from northern European countries tended to rate the academic progress abroad less positively than those from southern European countries. For example, 41 percent of Danish students rated their academic progress abroad lower than at home, compared with 19 percent of all ERASMUS students. On the other hand, 81 percent of Greek students - compared with 55 percent of all ERASMUS students - considered academic progress abroad more positively than that at home.

Correspondingly, those who spent the ERASMUS-supported study period in northern European countries rated the academic success during that period more positively than those who had spent that period in southern Europe. For example, 82 percent of those going to Denmark considered progress abroad to be higher. Ireland turned out to be an exception, for academic progress of ERASMUS students who spent their study period in Ireland, was - on the same level as by those going to Greece and Portugal, - the least favourably assessed.

Table 8.6
Academic Progress Abroad, by Country of Home University and Host Country (mean[1])

	Country of home university											Total
	B	D	DK	E	F	GR	I	IRL	NL	P	UK	
B	.	*	.	2.2	2.2	.	2.0	*	2.9	.	2.4	2.4
D	2.3	.	*	2.2	2.2	*	1.9	*	2.3	.	2.8	2.4
DK	*	*	.	*	*	*	.	.	1.7	.	2.0	1.8
E	2.1	2.8	.	.	2.2	.	2.5	*	2.6	*	2.7	2.5
F	2.6	2.7	*	2.1	.	*	2.1	2.6	2.3	*	2.8	2.6
GR	.	*	*	2.4	*	.	*	.	*	.	*	2.7
I	2.2	3.5	*	2.2	2.2	*	.	*	3.2	*	2.5	2.6
IRL	*	3.0	*	*	2.6	.	*	.	*	*	*	2.7
NL	2.3	2.5	*	*	2.5	*	1.9	*	.	.	2.7	2.4
P	*	*	.	*	2.5	.	*	*	*	.	*	2.7
UK	1.8	2.6	2.4	2.2	2.1	1.9	2.3	2.8	2.7	.	.	2.3
Total	2.3	2.7	2.9	2.2	2.2	1.7	2.2	2.8	2.6	2.3	2.7	2.5

[1] On a scale from 1 = "much better" to 5 = "much less"
* Figure not provided, because number of students responding was less than 10

Question 6.4: How would you rate your general academic progress during your study period abroad, compared with what you would have expected in a corresponding period at your home university?

In looking at the ratings both by country of home university and host country, we took into account only those home-host country directions of exchange in which at least ten students replied to the survey (49 of possible 110 home-host directions of exchange, see Table 8.6). On average, more positive ratings than 2.0 were given by Dutch students going to Denmark (1.7) and by Italian students going both to Germany and the Netherlands (1.9 each), whereas the most negative rating was found in the case of German students going to Italy (3.5). If we focus on the exchange between students of the three countries most strongly represented in the ERASMUS programme, we note that French students rated their academic success as more positive in Germany and the United Kingdom compared with academic success at home (2.6), whereas German students considered academic success in the United Kingdom (2.6) and France (2.7) and British students in France and Germany (2.8 each) only moderately more positive than at home.

Table 8.7
Academic Progress Abroad in Comparison to Study at Home University, by Field of Study (mean*)

	Academic progress abroad	
Major field (during study period abroad)	Mean*	n
Agricultural sciences	2.6	31
Architecture, urban and regional planning	2.6	101
Art and design	2.2	50
Business studies, management sciences	2.6	1037
Education, teacher training	2.6	39
Engineering, technology	2.6	309
Geography, geology	2.7	21
Humanities	2.6	112
Languages, philological sciences	2.2	562
Law	2.2	332
Mathematics, informatics	2.5	72
Medical sciences	2.3	45
Natural sciences	2.6	133
Social sciences	2.3	126
Communication and information sciences	2.2	14
Other areas of study	2.5	149
Total	2.5	3133

Question 6.4: How would you rate your general academic progress during your study period abroad, compared with what you would have expected in a corresponding period at your home university?
* On a scale from 1 = "much better" to 5 = "much less"

The ratings varied to some extent according to field of study, as Table 8.7 shows. As far as the fields most strongly represented in the ERASMUS programme were concerned, students of languages and law rated the academic progress abroad more positively than students in business and engineering. As regards the smaller fields, students of arts and design and those of communication and information sciences rated most positively.

8.7   Impediments to Academic Progress Abroad

Those who rated their academic progress abroad to be lower than at home, i.e. about one fifth of the ERASMUS students, were asked to state the major reasons. Of the nine categories provided, those mentioned most often were:
- differences in teaching, learning and examination modes between the host and the home university (46 % of those rating their academic progress abroad lower, i.e. 10 % of all ERASMUS students surveyed)
- substantial differences in course content (39 %, or 8 % of all respondents)
- lack of guidance and supervision (35 %, or 7 % of all students)
- organizational drawbacks, such as timing of courses and exams, accessibility of courses, etc. (29 %, or 6 % of all students).

Thus, clearly those reasons for limited academic success most frequently stated referred to educational discrepancies between higher education systems, or to the academic and organizational setting of the programme. Reasons which could be attributed to the students themselves seemed to have played a lesser role:
- language barriers (26 % of those rating their academic progress abroad lower than at home, or 5 % of all students)
- students themselves did not work well, i.e not hard enough, etc. (19 %, or 4 % of all)
- students' personal problems (12 %, or 2 % respectively)
- more demanding courses at host university (11 %, or 2 % of all students)
- students' difficulties of living abroad (8 %, or 2 % of all students).

The longer the duration of the study period abroad, the more students who reported less academic problems abroad, tended to state various other difficulties. Problems which related to academic and organizational dimensions of the programmes were most often named as impediments to academic progress abroad by Danish, British and Irish students, as Table 8.8 shows. Finally, it is worthwhile mentioning that language barriers were overproportionally often mentioned as a reason for low academic progress abroad by students going to Italy (10 % of all going to Italy), Portugal (8 %), Greece and France (7 % each).

Table 8.8
Reasons for less Academic Progress Abroad, by Host Country (mean*)

	Host country											Total
---	B	D	DK	E	F	GR	I	IRL	NL	P	UK	
Language barriers	16	27	50	25	32	38	38	14	26	33	17	26
Courses at host university more demanding	17	18	50	5	16	18	14	3	8	9	4	11
Content of courses substantially different	55	43	50	41	42	25	47	50	42	36	29	39
Teaching, learning, examination modes different	45	34	0	51	58	40	51	48	38	50	36	46
Organizational drawbacks	36	23	0	27	41	50	36	21	22	36	19	29
Lack of guidance, supervision, etc.	18	33	0	37	54	33	49	18	23	64	14	35
Personal problems	0	7	0	15	15	0	14	9	18	0	11	12
Difficulties of living abroad	5	4	0	5	10	0	15	9	8	8	7	8
Did not work well (not hard enough etc.)	14	21	0	16	22	9	19	23	21	0	19	19

Question 6.5: If your academic progress was worse abroad than you would have expected at your home university (4 or 5 in question 6.4), what role did the following factors play?

* Percent 1 + 2 on a scale from 1 = "played a very important role" to 5 = "did not play any role"

Chapter 9

Improvement of Foreign Language Proficiency and Cultural Impacts

9.1   The Scope of the Analysis

Pursuit of academic interests and academic achievement as well as improvement of career prospects are generally accepted as major motives for study in another country for some period. In fact, research has shown that many former participants of study abroad programmes perceived that the study period abroad had a positive impact on employment opportunities and various other aspects of career. A survey conducted in the eighties, however, showed that graduates perceived stronger linguistic and cultural impacts resulting from a study period abroad than academic and professional impacts.

In the framework of this study we could not establish the long-term impacts of a study period in another EC Member State. What was possible, though, was to elicit students' views regarding the progress of foreign language proficiency in the course of the study abroad period. Similarly, a few dimensions of cultural impacts were analysed: the knowledge acquired on many aspects of the host country's culture and society, and the change of opinions on various aspects both of the host and the home country.

One methodological problem should be briefly addressed in advance. Students were asked upon return to rate their foreign language proficiency, cultural knowledge and opinions of the host and home country both before and after the study period abroad. Thus, proficiencies, knowledge and attitudes prior to the sojourn were measured retrospectively. Retrospective surveys of this kind are criticized for creating artificially large measures of change, because respondents, believing that they have improved, might rate prior proficiencies lower and prior attitudes too negatively, thus underscoring their improvement. In the framework of the research project conducted in the mid-eighties already referred to, one cohort of students participating in the same programmes was asked retrospectively and the next cohort in a longitudinal setting, i.e. asked both before they went abroad and upon return. In fact, that study proved that the degree of change looks far more impressive in retrospective analysis than in a longitudinal analysis. These findings do not prove, however, that longitudinal measures are more valid than retrospective ones. For example, Students might note during the study abroad period, that they had overestimated their level of prior foreign language proficiency and the use they could make of this level. As a consequence, they might raise the standard as regards what is required for understanding a telephone conversation or an academic lecture, and therefore set a higher yardstick in rating the proficiency upon return. If this was true, a longitudinal setting would artificially diminish the improvement realized in the study abroad period, whereas a retrospective setting - a rating of the proficiencies before and after the study period both upon return - can be based, in principle, on an identical yardstick. We cannot prove the superiority of any of the two procedures in the framework of this study. Our option for a retrospective analysis was pragmatically based on the timing and the resources available; however, we assume that a retrospective analysis certainly can claim sufficient validity and might be actually superior to a longitudinal analysis.

9.2   Improvement of Foreign Language Proficiency

ERASMUS students were asked to rate their proficiency in the (major) language of instruction at the host university in three categories:
- reading, listening, speaking and writing
- separately in academic setting and outside classroom
- prior to the study period abroad and after the period abroad.

All 16 ratings were on a scale from 1= "very good" to 7 = "extremely limited". Excluded from the subsequent analysis were 11 percent of ERASMUS students, most of whom were taught completely or predominantly in their mother tongue while abroad, and some of those who did not provide complete ratings.

According to their ratings, ERASMUS students had a remarkable level of foreign language proficiency already, prior to the study abroad period. Average ratings ranged from 3.4 to 4.2, as Table 9.1 shows. Proficiency in academic settings was rated to be only slightly inferior to proficiency outside the classroom. Passive proficiency, i.e. reading and listening, was considered clearly better - about half a scale-point - than active proficiency, i.e. speaking and writing.

On average for the eight ratings, Greek ERASMUS students considered their proficiency in the major language taught abroad best (3.1), whereas Irish (4.4), Italian (4.3) and British (4.1) rated it lowest. The low proficiency of Irish and British students certainly reflects the fact that their home language is most widely used internationally and thus the need for foreign language learning seems to be less obvious. This corresponds to the fact that students who went to Ireland and to the United Kingdom rated their prior knowledge of the language of instruction at the host university highest (means of 3.4 and 3.5 across the eight ratings), as Table 9.2 indicates. Students going to Portugal (5.0), Italy, the Netherlands (4.5 each) and Belgium (4.4) felt least prepared with regards to proficiency in the host country language.

Students enrolled in foreign language studies as well as those in communication sciences felt strongest in the foreign language prior to the study period abroad, whereas students in architecture, fine arts, geography and geology, and engineering rated their prior foreign language proficiency modestly. It is worth reporting that students who went abroad immediately at the beginning of their first year of study reported the highest level of foreign language proficiency prior to the study abroad period (3.3 on average of the eight ratings compared with 3.8 for all students).

Table 9.1
Selfrating of Competency in Language of Instruction Prior and After Study Period Abroad, by Country of Home University (mean*)

		Country of home university											Total
		B	D	DK	E	F	GR	I	IRL	NL	P	UK	
Reading in academic setting	prior	3.3	3.3	3.3	3.3	3.5	3.2	2.7	3.9	4.1	3.5	3.2	3.5
	after	1.8	1.8	1.8	1.9	2.0	1.7	1.4	2.1	2.8	2.2	1.4	2.0
Listening in academic setting	prior	3.8	3.8	3.7	3.6	3.7	3.5	3.3	4.1	4.4	3.5	3.8	3.7
	after	1.9	1.9	1.8	1.9	1.9	1.8	1.8	2.2	2.9	2.1	1.6	1.9
Speaking in academic setting	prior	3.3	3.3	4.1	4.5	4.2	4.0	3.6	4.7	4.8	4.3	4.7	4.2
	after	2.3	2.3	2.2	2.7	2.4	2.2	2.2	2.7	3.2	2.7	1.9	2.4
Writing in academic setting	prior	4.0	4.0	3.9	4.5	4.1	3.8	3.2	4.8	4.7	4.2	5.3	4.1
	after	2.4	2.4	2.4	3.1	2.7	2.3	1.9	3.2	3.6	2.7	2.4	2.6
Reading outside classroom	prior	3.4	3.4	3.0	3.2	3.6	3.3	2.6	4.0	4.2	3.3	2.8	3.4
	after	1.8	1.8	1.7	1.8	2.1	1.8	1.6	2.1	3.0	2.0	1.3	2.0
Listening outside classroom	prior	3.9	3.9	3.4	3.4	3.9	3.7	3.4	4.2	4.2	3.3	3.5	3.7
	after	1.9	1.9	1.7	1.8	2.0	1.8	1.9	2.1	2.6	1.9	1.6	1.9
Speaking outside classroom	prior	4.1	4.1	3.7	3.8	4.1	3.8	3.2	4.4	4.5	3.6	4.1	4.0
	after	2.1	2.1	2.0	2.2	2.2	2.0	1.8	2.3	2.9	2.2	1.8	2.1
Writing outside classroom	prior	4.1	4.1	3.6	4.2	4.1	3.8	2.8	4.6	4.6	3.9	4.7	4.0
	after	2.3	2.3	2.3	2.7	2.6	2.2	1.8	2.9	3.7	2.7	2.1	2.5

Question 4.7: How do you rate your competency in the (major) language of instruction at the host university (reply only if different from the language of instruction at your home university)?

* On a scale from 1 = "very good" to 7 = "extremely limited"

Table 9.2
Selfrating of Competency in Language of Instruction Prior to After Study Period Abroad, by Host Country
(mean*)

		Host country												Total
		B	D	DK	E	F	GR	I	IRL	NL	P	UK		
Reading in academic setting	prior	3.9	3.5	3.9	3.5	3.4	4.3	3.2	4.0	4.4		3.1		3.5
	after	2.5	2.1	3.1	1.9	2.3	2.2	1.8	2.8	2.7		1.7		2.0
Listening in academic setting	prior	4.3	3.6	4.1	3.7	3.8	3.5	4.3	3.4	4.5	4.9	3.5		3.7
	after	2.6	2.0	3.0	1.9	2.0	2.2	2.1	1.8	3.0	2.7	1.8		1.9
Speaking in academic setting	prior	4.7	4.2	4.6	4.3	4.3	4.0	4.8	3.9	4.8	5.3	4.0		4.2
	after	3.1	2.5	3.5	2.3	2.4	2.8	2.7	2.1	3.4	3.6	2.2		2.4
Writing in academic setting	prior	4.7	4.1	4.6	4.1	4.2	4.1	4.9	3.8	4.7	4.9	3.7		4.1
	after	3.4	2.6	3.6	2.5	2.7	3.2	3.1	2.2	3.7	3.7	2.3		2.6
Reading outside classroom	prior	4.2	3.4	3.9	3.5	3.5	3.3	4.2	3.0	4.2	4.5	3.1		3.4
	after	2.7	2.0	2.9	1.9	2.0	2.4	2.1	1.7	2.9	2.6	1.8		2.0
Listening outside classroom	prior	4.5	3.4	4.1	3.8	3.8	3.5	4.2	3.2	4.5	5.3	3.5		3.7
	after	2.7	1.8	2.9	1.8	1.9	2.3	1.9	1.7	3.0	3.2	1.8		1.9
Speaking outside classroom	prior	4.5	3.7	4.3	4.1	4.1	3.9	4.5	3.4	4.8	5.4	3.7		4.0
	after	2.8	2.0	3.0	2.1	2.1	2.5	1.9	1.9	3.3	3.7	2.0		2.1
Writing outside classroom	prior	4.9	3.8	4.5	4.0	4.1	3.9	4.9	3.6	4.7	5.2	3.6		4.0
	after	3.2	2.4	3.4	2.4	2.6	2.9	2.9	2.2	3.7	3.6	2.2		2.5

Question 4.7: How do you rate your competency in the (major) language of instruction at the host university (reply only if different from the language of instruction at your home university)?

* On a scale from 1 = "very good" to 7 = "extremely limited"

The study abroad period proved effective in improving the level of foreign language proficiency to a substantial extent. Self-ratings improved on average from 3.8 to 2.2 on the seven-point-scale. Mean values for listening and reading were 1.9 and 2.0 after the study abroad period, both in an academic setting and outside the classroom. Speaking and writing remained somewhat less highly rated than listening and reading, but improved to about the same extent, as Table 9.1 shows. Speaking in an academic context (2.4) remained more cautiously assessed than speaking outside the classroom (2.1).

In analysing the conditions for improvement of foreign language proficiency during the study period abroad, we naturally turn to the duration of the study period in the host country. In fact, we note a clear positive correlation between duration and the foreign language improvement, although the improvement is not continuous. As Chart 9.1 shows, growth did not continue beyond seven months: passive proficiency reached a high level after four months, but "a ceiling" was reached for speaking and writing ability around seven months.

In addition, the level of prior foreign language competence seemed to be slightly negatively related to the improvement during the study abroad period. This can be shown, if we compare proficiencies prior to and after the study abroad period both by home country and by host country (see Tables 9.1 and 9.2) and calculate the increase on that basis. As regards home country, we note that students from those four countries who rated their foreign languages proficiency highest before the study abroad period, improved on average by 1.5, whereas students from countries who rated their proficiency lowest initially, improved by 1.7. Similarly, foreign language proficiency of guest students improved in those countries whose incoming students know the language relatively well (by 1.4 on average), whereas guest students in those countries where the proficiency of host language was relatively low before the study abroad period, improved by 1.7. Students less prepared for the host country language obviously improved slightly more, but not nearly to the extent of really balancing the differences. If the scales were valid in measuring equal distances, we could argue that of the differences by home country and host country existing prior to the study abroad, about a third was made up during the study period.

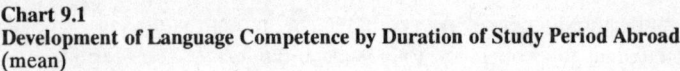

Chart 9.1
Development of Language Competence by Duration of Study Period Abroad
(mean)

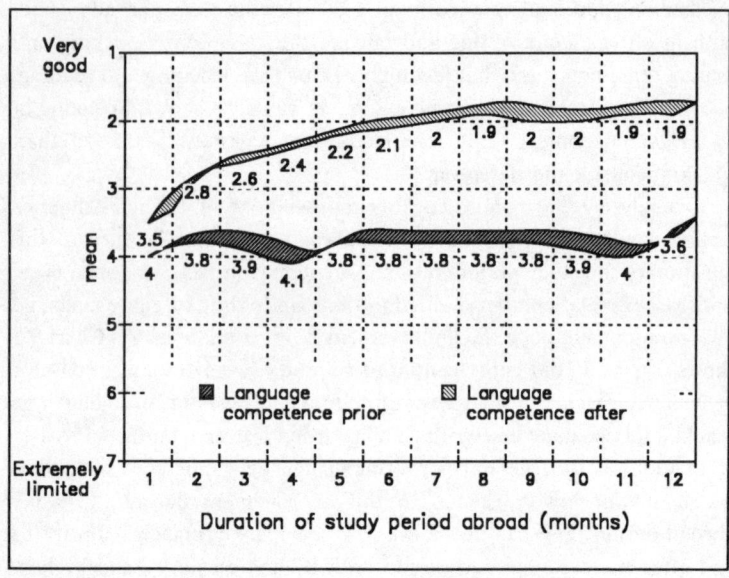

9.2   Knowledge about the Host Country

As in the case of foreign language proficiency, students were also asked
to rate their knowledge about the host country as it was, retrospectively
seen, immediately before and after the study period abroad ("now"). On
a scale from 1 = "extensive knowledge" to 5 = "very minimal knowledge", they were asked to rate 13 aspects, notably regarding politics,
culture and society, the economic system and the geography as well as
the higher education system of the host country.

ERASMUS students had, according to their retrospective self-rating,
a very low level of knowledge on the host country prior to the study
period. The ratings were 3.5 on average, with knowledge of geography,
the highest rated aspect, in the centre of the scale (3.0) between
"extensive" and "minimal" knowledge. The least knowledge was reported
on treatment of recently arrived immigrants (3.9) and on the system of

higher education of the host country (3.8). Altogether, replies to the various aspects were highly correlated (ranging from 0.30 to 0.76) both before and after the study abroad period. This suggests that levels of knowledge of the host country differed much more between students than between the different aspects of knowledge i.e. if students were well informed, they tended to be so about all aspects.

Knowledge of the host country prior to the study period abroad did not differ strongly according to the country of the home university, as Table 9.3 shows. Greek (3.0 on average) and Portuguese students (3.6) were very knowledgeable of the host country, whereas Italian (3.7) and British students (3.6) rated their prior knowledge of the host country lowest. Students who went to Germany considered themselves the best informed about the host country (3.2 on average), whereas those going to Denmark (4.3), Portugal (4.2), Greece or Ireland (3.9 each) felt themselves least informed. Obviously prior knowledge of the "smaller" countries of the EC was limited.

Male and female ERASMUS students reported more or less the same level of knowledge of the host country, both prior to and after the study abroad period. There were also no indications that those going abroad for relatively long periods were better prepared for their stay in the host country, as far as prior knowledge on culture and society, politics or the economic system was concerned. As regards fields of study, we finally note that students in agriculture, architecture, mathematics (3.9 on average) and fine arts (3.8) rated their knowledge lowest, whereas those enrolled in communication science rated their prior knowledge highest (3.1). As one might expect, students were better informed on those aspects of the host country which closely related to their field of expertise, such as students of geography and geology on the geography of the host country (2.6 compared with 3.0 on average of all students).

Upon return from the study abroad period, students rated their knowledge of the host country much higher. The average score of 2.3 indicates an average improvement by 1.2 on the five-point scale. Highest improvement was reported regarding higher education (1.9) and above-average improvement regarding cultural and social issues (except for treatment of recently arrived immigrants), while knowledge on political issues and the geography of the host country increased to a lesser extent.

Table 5.3
Selfrating of Knowledge About Host Country Before Study Period Abroad and Now, by Country of Home University (mean*)

		Country of home university											Total
		B	D	DK	E	F	GR	I	IRL	NL	P	UK	
Political system and institutions	before	3.4	3.4	3.1	3.6	3.4	2.8	3.8	3.6	3.7	3.1	3.7	3.5
	now	2.4	2.1	1.9	2.4	2.3	1.8	2.4	2.3	2.3	1.8	2.5	2.3
Dominant political issues	before	3.4	3.6	3.2	3.6	3.6	3.1	3.9	3.5	3.6	2.8	3.8	3.6
	now	2.5	2.0	1.9	2.4	2.3	1.8	2.4	2.4	2.4	1.8	2.5	2.3
Foreign policy in general	before	3.4	3.3	3.1	3.3	3.4	2.9	3.6	3.5	3.6	2.9	3.9	3.5
	now	2.8	2.3	2.2	2.5	2.5	2.0	2.6	2.5	2.7	2.2	2.9	2.6
Policy towards your own country	before	3.5	3.3	3.4	3.1	3.1	2.5	3.6	3.5	3.8	3.2	3.8	3.4
	now	3.0	2.3	2.8	2.4	2.3	1.9	2.6	2.4	3.1	2.5	2.7	2.5
System of higher education	before	4.0	3.8	3.6	4.0	3.8	3.6	4.0	3.8	3.9	3.4	3.6	3.8
	now	2.1	1.8	2.0	1.9	1.9	1.7	2.1	2.0	2.2	1.4	2.0	1.9
Cultural life (art, music, theatre, etc.)	before	3.2	3.3	3.4	3.5	3.5	2.9	3.4	3.2	3.2	3.0	3.4	3.4
	now	2.3	1.9	2.1	2.2	2.2	2.0	2.1	2.1	2.3	1.4	2.0	2.1
Dominant social issues	before	3.5	3.6	3.6	3.6	3.6	3.3	3.6	3.5	3.4	3.2	3.6	3.6
	now	2.5	2.1	2.3	2.2	2.3	2.1	2.1	2.1	2.3	1.7	2.3	2.2
Economic system	before	3.3	3.2	3.1	3.5	3.3	2.9	3.8	3.4	3.5	2.7	3.8	3.4
	now	2.7	2.2	2.2	2.6	2.3	2.1	2.6	2.3	2.7	1.8	2.8	2.5
The countrys geography (to be cont.)	before	3.0	2.8	2.7	3.3	3.1	2.8	3.1	3.2	3.2	2.5	3.1	3.0
	now	2.1	1.8	1.7	2.0	1.9	1.8	1.9	2.0	2.1	1.5	1.9	1.9

(Table 9.3 cont.)

						Country of home university							Total
		B	D	DK	E	F	GR	I	IRL	NL	P	UK	
Social structure family, class system)	before	3.3	3.3	3.2	3.4	3.3	3.1	3.6	3.1	3.4	3.4	3.4	3.4
	now	2.3	2.0	1.9	2.2	2.2	1.8	2.1	1.9	2.2	2.1	2.2	2.1
Customs, traditions, religion	before	3.2	3.3	3.4	3.4	3.3	3.0	3.5	3.0	3.3	3.0	3.3	3.3
	now	2.1	1.9	2.0	2.0	2.0	1.9	2.1	1.8	2.2	1.7	2.1	2.0
Treatment of recently arrived immigrants	before	3.8	3.8	3.5	3.8	4.0	3.6	4.0	3.7	3.7	4.1	3.8	3.9
	now	2.8	2.5	2.3	2.4	2.8	2.1	2.5	2.2	2.7	2.9	2.5	2.6
Sports, leisure/ recreational activities	before	3.3	3.4	3.7	3.5	3.4	2.9	3.7	3.3	3.5	3.2	3.6	3.5
	now	2.5	2.2	2.1	2.3	2.1	1.9	2.3	2.3	2.6	1.7	2.4	2.3

Question 6.2: How would you rate your level of knowledge with regard to the following aspects of the host country, immediately before you went abroad and now?

* On a scale from 1 = "extensive knowledge" to 5 = "very minimal knowledge"

The degree of increased knowledge of the host country upon return was strongly related to the duration of study, as Table 9.4 shows in detail. Those students who had spent up to two months abroad, rated their knowledge on the host country 2.7 on average, those spending three months 2.4, those four to six months 2.3, and those seven to twelve months 2.2. As those staying more than a year reported 2.0 on average, one might state that more time is needed than supported by the ERASMUS programme in order to acquire a "good" knowledge of the host country.

Differences regarding the knowledge of the various host countries were marginal after the study abroad period. If we aggregate the responses to the various aspects, we note that only the knowledge on Portugal clearly remained below average; the gap between various host countries, however, was lower upon return than it was prior to the study abroad period. Before the study abroad period, the average scores between the three best known and the three worst known countries differed by 0.8, whereas the respective difference was 0.3 upon return. The gap of knowledge on "small" and "big" host countries clearly decreased during the study period abroad.

On the other hand, differences in the knowledge of the host country which could be observed according to the home country of the students prior to the study abroad, remained more or less stable. For example, Greek and Portuguese students who stated the highest knowledge of the host country before the sojourn, did so again after the study period abroad (1.9 on average each). Also, most differences observed prior to the study abroad period regarding the field of study remained more or less stable, though students from those fields stating the least knowledge before the study abroad period also narrowed that gap to some extent. Above-average improvement was frequently noticeable in areas of knowledge associated to the respective field.

In looking at the individual aspects of knowledge, we also note that the differences of average ratings of the hosting countries were much smaller upon return than prior to the study abroad period. After the study abroad period, differences in knowledge of the host country were only remarkable regarding two aspects: the host country's policy on the students' own country and the treatment of recently arrived immigrant groups. In both cases, knowledge remained lower in small host countries.

Table 9.4
Selfrating of Knowledge About Host Country After Study Period Abroad, by Duration of Study Period Abroad (mean*)

	Duration of Study Abroad					
	1-2 months	3 months	4-6 months	7-12 months	13 and more months	Total
Political system and institutions	2.6	2.5	2.3	2.2	1.9	2.3
Dominant political issues	2.7	2.5	2.3	2.2	1.9	2.3
Foreign policy in general	3.1	2.8	2.5	2.5	2.2	2.6
Policy towards your own country	3.2	2.7	2.6	2.4	2.0	2.5
System of higher education	2.6	2.1	2.0	1.8	1.7	1.9
Cultural life (art, music, theatre, etc.)	2.5	2.1	2.1	2.0	2.0	2.1
Dominant social issues	2.7	2.3	2.2	2.2	2.1	2.2
Economic system	3.0	2.7	2.4	2.4	1.9	2.5
The countrys geography	2.1	1.9	1.9	1.8	1.8	1.9
Social structure (family, class system)	2.7	2.3	2.1	2.1	1.9	2.1
Customs, traditions, religion	2.5	2.1	2.0	2.0	1.9	2.0
Treatment of recently arrived immigrants	3.2	2.8	2.6	2.4	2.5	2.6
Sports, leisure/ recreational activities	2.9	2.4	2.3	2.1	2.1	2.3

Question 6.2: How would you rate your level of knowledge with regard to the following aspects of the host country, immediately before you went abroad and after?

* On a scale from 1 = "extensive knowledge" to 5 = "very minimal knowledge"

9.3 Opinions of Culture and Society

Students' opinions of a host country, their people, culture, politics and ·living conditions, might range from xenophobia to excited praise. One might hope that knowledge and experience would dissolve stereotypes, but this does not necessarily lead to more positive opinions. Empathy might grow along with experience, but other attitudes might become more negative in the process of discovering problems about which a foreigner not having lived in that country is usually oblivious. Opinions might become more diverse regarding different aspects as the knowledge base improves. Finally, opinions on the home country might become more positive or negative, depending on the experiences abroad, on the ways the individual coped with life and study abroad, or on the ways a period abroad stimulated reflections on one's home country[1].

ERASMUS students were asked to rate their opinions on the host country and on the home country both immediately before, retrospectively, and after the study period abroad in respect to eight aspects, such as foreign policy, cultural life and the higher education system. Again, a five-point scale was provided from 1 = "highly positive" to 5 = "highly negative". The questions raised as regards opinion differ from those raised regarding knowledge in one respect: as regards opinion, a comparison is possible of the views on the host country to that on the home country. The formulation of the question is identical to that in the previously mentioned study conducted in the mid-eighties. That study came to the conclusions that the individual students' opinions on the home and host country frequently changed and became more specific due to knowledge acquired on various aspects, but that opinions hardly changed on average across students. If small differences are taken into account, an average change towards a slightly more negative attitude regarding the host country and a slightly more positive attitude regarding the home country could be observed.

Altogether, we also note that ERASMUS students' opinions about the host country neither become clearly more positive nor clearly more negative (see Tables 9.5 and 9.6). The average rating of all aspects across all host countries was 2.9 before the study period abroad, and improved marginally (not statistically significant) by 0.05. The opinions about the home country were on average (2.9) the same before the study abroad as about the host country, and they also improved to the same, statistically not significant, extent of 0.05. Changes of opinions both on the home and host country cannot be explained either by differing

---

[1]   Cf. Opper/Teichler/Carlson 1990, chapter 6.3.

durations of the study period.

Altogether, the cultural life in the host country was most highly appreciated, while opinions on the host country's treatments of immigrants and environmental policies were most negative. Opinions on the home country were similar on average to those of the host country, except for more positive ratings of the home country's foreign policies and more negative ratings of the home country's cultural life.

Factor analyses of the opinions voiced show separate dimensions of opinions on home country politics, society and culture. As regards opinions on the host country no clear patterns emerge, regarding either the opinions voiced before or after the study period abroad.

A substantial number of students stated before the study abroad period that they did not yet have any opinion about their host country. On average of the nine items, this was stated in 21 percent of the cases before the study abroad period and in six percent of the cases upon return. Before the study abroad period, proportions of "do not know" statements ranged from 32 percent regarding treatment of immigrants to 12 percent regarding cultural life, while about a quarter had not yet developed an opinion on the various political aspects. After the study abroad period, "do not know" was most often stated regarding political aspects. The longer the period abroad, the less often students stated "do not know" upon return.

Opinions on the respective host countries varied substantially according to the individual aspects. For example, the Danish higher education system (1.8) was most favourably assessed after the study period by the students who had spent the ERASMUS-supported period there, an average improvement in assessment of 0.5. The German system of higher education was rated second highest by the guest students (2.2), an assessment which was not different on average from those before the period of study in the Federal Republic of Germany. German students viewed higher education in their home country somewhat more critically (2.5 and 2.6), i.e. exactly the mean of all ERASMUS students' rating their respective home higher education system. German ERASMUS students, however, gave lowest marks to the higher education systems of their respective host countries (2.9 prior to the study period abroad and 3.0 on return).

Table 9.5
Opinions About Host Country Before Study Abroad, by Host Country (mean*)

	Host country											Total
	B	D	DK	E	F	GR	I	IRL	NL	P	UK	
Post-secondary/higher education in host country	2.5	2.2	2.3	3.1	2.7	2.7	2.9	2.7	2.6	3.1	2.6	2.6
Foreign policy in host country	2.8	2.7	2.8	3.0	3.0	3.2	3.0	3.0	2.7	3.0	3.4	3.1
Cultural life in host country	2.7	2.6	2.8	2.4	2.7	2.6	2.2	2.6	2.6	3.0	2.7	2.5
Media in host country	2.8	2.8	2.6	2.9	2.8	2.7	3.0	3.1	2.8	3.2	2.8	2.8
Customs and traditions in host country	2.9	2.7	2.8	2.3	2.6	2.9	2.5	2.6	2.9	2.8	2.8	2.7
Treatment of recently arr. immigrants in host country	3.0	3.4	2.8	3.0	3.5	3.0	3.1	3.2	2.7	3.2	3.2	3.3
Social structure in host country	2.9	2.8	2.8	3.0	3.0	3.0	2.9	3.2	2.8	3.3	3.2	3.0
Urban life in host country	2.6	2.7	2.9	2.8	2.9	3.1	2.8	3.1	2.7	2.9	3.0	2.8
Governmental domestic policies in host country	3.0	2.8	3.2	3.1	3.0	3.2	3.4	3.3	2.8	3.2	3.4	3.1
Environmental policies in host country	3.1	2.2	2.4	3.8	3.4	3.2	3.7	3.3	2.4	3.4	3.5	3.3

Question 6.3: What was your opinion about each of the following aspects of the host country and the home country immediately before you went abroad? And what is your opinion now?

* On a scale from 1 = "highly positive opinion" to 5 = "highly negative opinion"

Table 9.6
Opinions About Host Country Before Study Abroad and Now, by Country of Home University (mean*)

		Country of home university											Total
		B	D	DK	E	F	GR	I	IRL	NL	P	UK	
Post-secondary/higher education in host c.	before	2.8	2.9	2.5	2.1	2.6	1.9	2.3	2.6	2.8	2.8	2.7	2.6
	now	2.6	3.0	2.7	2.4	2.4	2.1	2.4	2.6	2.7	2.8	2.8	2.7
Foreign policy in host country	before	2.9	3.2	3.0	3.0	3.2	2.9	3.2	3.3	3.2	3.0	3.0	3.1
	now	2.8	3.3	3.1	3.0	3.1	3.1	3.1	3.2	3.1	2.3	2.8	3.1
Cultural life in host country	before	2.6	2.6	2.5	2.4	2.6	2.4	2.5	2.6	2.5	2.4	2.5	2.5
	now	2.3	2.3	2.0	2.2	2.2	2.3	2.2	2.0	2.2	1.7	2.1	2.2
Media in host country	before	2.8	2.8	2.9	2.3	2.8	2.5	2.9	3.1	3.0	2.5	3.0	2.8
	now	2.6	2.8	2.8	2.2	2.6	2.4	3.0	3.0	3.0	2.3	2.9	2.7
Customs and traditions in host country	before	2.8	2.7	2.7	2.8	2.6	2.6	2.6	2.6	2.8	2.6	2.6	2.7
	now	2.6	2.4	2.4	2.5	2.3	2.5	2.4	2.2	2.4	2.3	2.2	2.4
Treatm. of recently arrived immigrants in host	before	3.0	3.3	3.2	3.3	3.1	3.0	3.4	3.6	3.3	2.8	3.4	3.3
	now	2.7	3.5	3.1	3.3	3.1	2.7	3.2	3.6	3.5	3.3	3.6	3.3
Social structure in host country	before	2.9	3.1	3.1	3.0	2.9	2.8	3.0	2.9	3.1	3.0	3.0	3.0
	now	2.9	3.3	3.2	3.0	3.0	2.9	3.0	2.9	2.9	2.6	2.8	3.0
Urban life in host country	before	2.9	2.8	2.8	2.9	2.8	2.6	2.7	3.3	2.8	3.0	2.9	2.8
	now	2.7	2.8	2.5	2.7	2.7	2.3	2.4	2.9	2.5	2.1	2.7	2.7
Governm. domestic policies in host country	before	3.0	3.2	3.3	3.1	3.2	2.9	3.2	3.4	3.4	2.5	3.0	3.1
	now	3.0	3.5	3.4	3.1	3.3	2.9	3.1	2.9	3.5	2.9	2.9	3.2
Environmental policies in host country	before	2.9	4.0	3.8	2.8	2.9	2.6	2.9	3.3	3.7	3.4	2.9	3.3
	now	2.8	4.4	3.8	2.6	2.9	2.3	2.8	3.1	3.8	3.1	2.8	3.3

Question 6.3: What was your opinion about each of the following aspects of the host country and the home country immediately before you went abroad? And what is your opinion now?

* On a scale from 1 = "highly positive opinion" to 5 = "highly negative opinion"

Customs and traditions in Spain and Portugal were most highly appreciated by guest students after the study abroad period. Urban life was considered - upon return - most agreeable in Denmark (2.1) and least attractive in Greece (3.2), Portugal (3.0) and the United Kingdom (2.9). German (1.8), Danish (1.9) and Dutch (2.0) environmental policies were rated very positively upon return, while ratings of environmental policies of other countries were viewed far more negatively (3.3 to 4.0). Regarding those aspects, similar differences were noted by the home students of the respective countries, though the differences of the ratings to that of students from others countries were much smaller.

As already noted, a longer duration of the study period did not lead to more positive ratings of the host country on average. Only the media were more positively assessed, the longer the stay in the host country. Female students did not significantly differ from men in their opinions on the home and host country.

The presentation of mean scores might suggest a stability of opinions not very much touched by experiences. If we analyze, however, the frequency of changes of opinions, we can observe dynamic developments. An average of all ratings regarding the host country shows:

- 22 percent more positive ratings after the study period than before the stay abroad
- 16 percent more negative ratings after the study abroad period
- 46 percent identical ratings before and after the study period abroad
- 16 percent ratings upon return had no corresponding ratings before the study period abroad. The students stated "do not know".

We note for example that opinions most often change regarding the higher education system of the host country, i.e. an area in which all students had first-hand experience; only a quarter of the students kept their opinions stable in this area. Altogether, changes of attitudes in the positive direction took place most often by students who spent their study period abroad in Ireland and Portugal, whereas changes in the negative direction occured most often among students who went to France.

Opinions about the home country remained much more stable. On average, 69 percent of the ratings remained unchanged, whereas 18 percent were more positive and 13 percent more negative upon return than prior to the study period abroad. In view of the fact that most students had spent almost all their life in the country of the home university, 31 percent changes of ratings of the home country might be considered to be remarkably high. Again, most changes of attitudes took place regarding the system of higher education. Thus, the in-depth experience of higher education in the host country caused in many cases a reconsideration of the strengths and weaknesses of higher education at home. Greek and Portuguese students changed their view on higher education in their home country most often in a positive direction, whereas French students considered the higher education system at home most often more negatively upon return.

Altogether we might state that study in another EC Member State was instrumental in changing opinions on many aspects of the host country, and to some extent on the home country as well. This did not lead, however, on average to more positive or more negative attitudes towards the host country or the home country. The value of the study period abroad regarding opinions was not to increase sympathy towards other countries or towards one's home country in general, but rather to provide opportunities for a broad range of experiences which might lead to changes of opinions in many respects.

Chapter 10

Comprehensive Assessment by the Participating Students

10.1 Personal Value of Study Abroad

Students were asked to state the extent to which they considered it worthwhile to study abroad taking into consideration such aspects as study progress, career, foreign language proficiency, understanding the host country, travel, or break from usual surroundings. They were asked to rate each of the ten aspects provided in the question on a scale from 1 = "extremely worthwhile" to 5 = "not at all worthwhile".

Altogether, students considered the study abroad period supported by the ERASMUS programme as worthwhile. The average rating for all ten aspects was 1.8, i.e. higher than scale point 2 which could be called "worthwhile".

Most positively assessed were cultural and foreign language outcomes:
- acquaintance with people in another country (1.4)
- knowledge and understanding of the host country (1.5)
- foreign language proficiency (1.6).

The opportunity to widen personal experience and to enhance career prospects were also highly regarded:
- opportunity to travel (1.7)
- break from usual surroundings (1.7)
- career prospects (1.8).

Contrasting learning experiences, new views on the home country and finally subsequent academic progress were appreciated as well, though

with somewhat less enthusiasm:
- other teaching methods than at home (1.9)
- new perspectives on home country (2.1)
- exposure to subjects not offered at home university (2.4)
- study progress after return (2.5).

A similar question on the value of the study abroad period had been asked in the previously mentioned survey conducted in the mid-eighties. The rank order of items according to the value the ERASMUS students placed on them turned out to be almost identical to that of the former Joint Study Programme students. Also, the mean scores were almost the same.

If we exclude foreign language proficiency, because of the uneven role the various foreign languages play in Europe, there were some differences in the value placed on having studied in certain host countries. The mean rating across the nine remaining categories differed moderately among host countries. It ranged from 1.8 by those who went to the Federal Republic of Germany and Denmark to 2.1 and 2.3 for students going to Greece and Portugal respectively.

Those countries least appreciated for the academic and professional value of studying there, i.e. Portugal (2.9 on average for the four respective items), Greece (2.5), Ireland (2.4), and Spain (2.3), in contrast to 1.9 in the case of Denmark and 2.0 of the Federal Republic of Germany, were much more favourably assessed in terms of the cultural values and experience. Spain, Italy, Germany and Ireland (1.4) were most favourably viewed in those respects with the Netherlands (1.8), Belgium and Portugal (1.7 each) least favourably.

The assessment of the value of the study abroad period varied, as expected, somewhat less according to home country than according to host country (see Table 10.2). Spanish students rated the study period abroad most positively (1.7 on average for 9 items), whereas students from Belgium, Germany, Portugal, Denmark and the Netherlands (2.1 to 2.0) were slightly more reserved in their judgements. As in the case of the rating concerning academic progress abroad (cf. Chapter 8), we note - with a few exceptions - a slight North-South gap, with northern European higher education systems more highly assessed and southern European higher education systems less highly.

Table 10.1
Personal Value of Study Abroad, by Host Country (mean*)

	Host country											Total
	B	D	DK	E	F	GR	I	IRL	NL	P	UK	
Other teaching methods than at home	2.0	1.9	1.7	2.3	2.0	2.2	2.0	2.3	1.8	2.6	1.7	1.9
Exposure to subject not offered at home university	2.0	2.2	1.8	2.6	2.3	2.7	2.4	2.7	2.7	3.0	2.4	2.4
Study progress after return	2.5	2.3	2.3	2.3	2.5	2.8	2.6	2.5	2.5	3.1	2.6	2.5
Opportunity to travel	1.8	1.6	1.5	1.5	1.7	1.6	1.4	1.5	1.9	1.6	1.7	1.7
Career prospects	2.3	1.7	1.9	1.8	1.7	2.4	1.8	2.1	2.1	2.8	1.7	1.8
Acquaintance with people in another country	1.6	1.4	1.7	1.2	1.5	1.3	1.4	1.4	1.6	1.6	1.4	1.4
Foreign language proficiency	1.6	1.3	2.5	1.3	1.3	1.8	1.3	1.4	2.1	1.8	1.3	1.4
New perspectives on home country	2.5	2.1	2.4	2.0	2.0	2.5	2.1	2.3	2.5	2.8	2.0	2.1
Knowledge and understanding of the host country	1.8	1.4	1.6	1.4	1.6	1.5	1.4	1.5	1.8	1.7	1.5	1.5
Break from usual surroundings	1.7	1.4	1.5	1.6	1.7	1.5	1.6	1.8	1.7	1.9	1.8	1.7

Question 6.7: To what extent do you consider it was worthwhile for you to study abroad with regard to the following aspects?

* On a scale from 1 = "extremly worthwhile" to 5 = "not at all worthwhile"

Table 10.2
Personal Value of Study Abroad, by Country of Home University (mean*)

	Country of home university											Total
	B	D	DK	E	F	GR	I	IRL	NL	P	UK	
Other teaching methods than at home	1.9	1.9	2.6	1.5	1.9	1.6	1.7	2.1	1.9	1.5	2.3	1.9
Exposure to subject not offered at home university	2.3	2.6	2.4	1.8	2.7	2.1	2.1	1.9	2.3	2.7	2.4	2.4
Study progress after return	2.6	2.7	2.5	2.3	2.5	2.2	2.5	2.4	2.5	2.9	2.3	2.5
Opportunity to travel	2.0	2.0	2.4	1.4	1.5	1.7	1.4	1.7	1.9	1.9	1.4	1.7
Career prospects	2.0	1.7	1.6	1.9	1.7	1.8	2.3	1.5	2.1	1.4	1.6	1.8
Acquaintance with people in another country	1.7	1.4	1.4	1.3	1.3	1.7	1.5	1.5	1.5	2.8	1.4	1.4
Foreign language proficiency	1.6	1.4	1.4	1.3	1.4	1.3	1.3	1.7	1.5	1.1	1.4	1.4
New perspectives on home country	2.6	1.9	2.5	2.0	2.1	2.0	2.5	2.0	2.5	1.7	2.1	2.1
Knowledge and understanding of the host country	1.9	1.5	1.5	1.5	1.4	1.7	1.6	1.7	1.6	1.5	1.5	1.5
Break from usual surroundings	1.5	2.3	1.4	1.4	1.3	1.5	1.5	1.5	1.6	2.6	1.5	1.7

Question 6.7: To what extent do you consider it was worthwhile for you to study abroad with regard to the following aspects?

* On a scale from 1 = "extremly worthwhile" to 5 = "not at all worthwhile"

The longer the duration of the study period, the more favourably it was rated (see Table 10.3). The average ratings for nine items (except foreign language proficiency) were 2.2 for students who had been abroad for at most two months, 2.0 in the case of a period of three months, 1.9 for those going abroad 4-6 months, 1.8 in the case of 7-12 months, and finally 1.7 in the case of a period of more than one year.

Table 10.3
Personal Value of Study Abroad, by Duration of Study Period Abroad (mean*)

	Duration of Study Abroad					
	1-2 months	3 months	4-6 months	7-12 months	13 and more months	Total
Other teaching methods than at home	2.2	2.0	1.9	1.9	1.8	1.9
Exposure to subj. not offered at home university	2.5	2.4	2.3	2.4	2.8	2.4
Study progress after return	2.7	2.6	2.5	2.4	2.5	2.5
Opportunity to travel	1.7	1.5	1.7	1.7	1.7	1.7
Career prospects	2.4	2.1	1.9	1.6	1.3	1.8
Acquaintance with people in another country	1.8	1.4	1.5	1.4	1.3	1.4
Foreign language proficiency	2.3	1.8	1.6	1.3	1.3	1.6
New perspectives on home country	2.6	2.4	2.2	1.9	1.6	2.1
Knowledge and understanding of the host country	1.9	1.6	1.6	1.4	1.3	1.5
Break from usual surroundings	2.1	1.6	1.7	1.6	1.5	1.7

Question 6.7: To what extent do you consider it was worthwhile for you to study abroad with regard to the following aspects?

* On a scale from 1 = "extremly worthwhile" to 5 = "not at all worthwhile"

Differences in the assessment of the value of the study abroad period were relatively small, as far as fields of study are concerned. Students of geography and geology and those of communication and information sciences (both 2.2) valued the study abroad period slightly lower than students of other fields of study. In addition, we note that students of agricultural fields, architecture, geography and geology most appreciated the opportunity to travel abroad (1.4 compared with 1.7 on average). Students of architecture and of geography and geology exposed the biggest gap in a comparatively cautious assessment of the academic and professional value of study abroad on the one hand and on the other a relatively positive assessment of the cultural and experience value of study abroad. Finally, students of business fields valued the study abroad period highly for the expected enhancement of their career prospects (1.4 compared with 1.8 on average).

10.2   Satisfaction with the Period Abroad

Asked to rate their satisfaction with their study abroad period ("all things considered") on a scale from 1 = "very satisfied" to 5 = "not satisfied at all", ERASMUS students rated 1.5 on average. This was even slightly more positive than the respective rating of Joint Study Programme students surveyed in the mid-eighties (1.7).

Table 10.4
Satisfaction with Study Period Abroad, by Host Country (mean*)

	Host country											Total
	B	D	DK	E	F	GR	I	IRL	NL	P	UK	
Satisfaction with study period abroad	1.6	1.3	1.4	1.4	1.6	1.4	1.6	1.5	1.6	1.9	1.4	1.5
(n)	(93)	(358)	(31)	(310)	(826)	(40)	(206)	(108)	(183)	(39)	(945)	3139

Question 6.8: All things considered, are you satisfied with your study period abroad?
* On a scale from 1 = "very satisfied" to 5 = "very dissatisfied"

Engineering (1.3) and law students (1.4) were most satisfied with the study abroad period. Some reservations were voiced by students of geography and geology (1.8) and of architecture, as well as of communication and information sciences (1.7), i.e. those fields in which students had expressed some reservation regarding the academic and professional value of the study period abroad.

Differences according to home or host country, to duration and to fields of study were relatively small and can only be discussed with some caution. Students going to the Federal Republic of Germany were most satisfied (1.3), closely followed, as Table 10.4 shows, by all other countries (1.4-1.6), except for Portugal (1.9). As regards home country, average ratings ranged only from 1.3 (Spain and France) to 1.7 (United Kingdom and Ireland), thus confirming again the North-South variation discussed before.

10.3   Most Striking Experiences during the Study Period Abroad

At the end of the questionnaire, the ERASMUS students were asked three questions about "the worst thing that happened to you while you were abroad", "the best thing that happened to you while you were abroad", and "the most difficult thing you successfully accomplished while you were abroad". The subsequent overview of responses, lists the answers most frequently given.

Problems ("worst things") mentioned most often referred to issues of accommodation. Almost 20 percent referred to accommodation problems (problems of search, quality of accommodation, problems with other people living in the same house, etc.) - an extraordinarily high quota in the case of an open question posed.

> "For the first month I lived in an awful, dark, damp flat which was overpriced and miles away from the university. Also this flat had no hot water in the kitchen, a fridge that didn't work and a landlord that tried to rip me and my friends off when we wanted to move. The only reason we stayed there was because we were new in town and desperate" (male English student who was in Spain).

Ten percent of the students also mentioned issues of accommodation in response to the question regarding the most difficult thing successfully accomplished.

"It was a big problem to find an adequate (and unexpensive) flat. I finally succeeded with a lot of help from friends" (Spanish student who was in Germany).

"The most difficult thing was to find within five days a permanent (and proper) accommodation" (German student who was in the United Kingdom).

Experience of crime and violence was mentioned second most often as a problem. Altogether, seven percent of the ERASMUS students referred to this problem. Some students were robbed during their stay abroad. In most cases in which crime and violence was mentioned as the worst experience during the study abroad period, students were not affected directly by criminal activities and violence in terms of robberies, but felt unsafe, like the female student who was in Ireland:

"The permanent fear for crime in Ireland, especially in Dublin, with regard to car thefts and pocket robberies"

"The crime rate in the host city was very high. I was not used to being permanently on guard" (male Danish student who was in the United Kingdom).

Some female students felt or observed sexual discrimination:

"There was a lot of sexual harassment from immigrants with completely different mentality" (female British student who was in France).

"I was shocked by the brutality of men against women in the public" (female German student who was in France).

Various negative characteristics of the host country and their people in general were named by five percent of ERASMUS students as the worst thing they experienced. Some examples might illustrate these third most frequently named negative experiences:

"I had difficulties in adopting the British way of life. The climate was unbearable. I felt very lonely; English people, though they are very, very kind are not friendly. Once we had a meeting in my room with friends from my own country, we made some noise but it was a Friday night and everybody seemed to be out. Next day I received a warning that they were going to throw me out of the university accommodation and that I wouldn't be able to find another room in any other accommodation" (female Greek student who was in the United Kingdom).

"I met a majority of Catalans who refused to talk to foreign university staff as well as students" (female French student who was in Spain).

"The worst experience was to see that the religious conflict between Catholics and Protestants was taking place in Scotland, too" (male Dutch student who was in the United Kingdom).

As regards the most positive experiences, more than half of the students praised the opportunity of getting acquainted with people - mostly from the host country, but from other countries as well. For example:

"The best experience was the hospitality and the helpfulness of the Greeks and the many contacts and discussions about policy and society" (male German student who was in Greece).

"The best thing that happened was the contact with the host family. I was received as the 13th child in the family and participated in their cultural and family life" (male Belgian student who was in the Netherlands).

"The best experience was that I met many foreign students and students from the host country who helped me when I had a lot of problems" (male Spanish student who was in France).

More than a quarter of the ERASMUS students considered the opportunity of getting to know the host country and its culture and society as the best thing they experienced during the study abroad period, such as:

"Meeting some super people and being able to travel and visit other places in Italy and also the rest of the continent" (female British student who was in Italy).

Academic experiences were named by about 10 percent of the students as the best thing that happened to them. As in response to the "closed" question about worthwhile experiences, academic experiences were not as favourably assessed here as personal contacts and cultural experiences.

Academic experiences, however, were in the forefront of reports by the students as regards the most difficult thing they achieved during the study period abroad. 30 percent of the ERASMUS students referred to academic issues in this context:

"The biggest difficulty I was confronted with was of an academic nature. It was a problem for me to get used to a higher education system different from the Spanish system with a reduced number of tasks but a special French methodology" (female Spanish student who was in France).

"The most difficult thing was to meet all academic requirements under pressure of time" (male German student who was in the United Kingdom).

"I took a seminar on a difficult topic which was attended by both students and lecturers. Being well reviewed boosted my confidence. I also got a lot of helpful feedback from the group" (male English student who was in Italy).

About 20 percent of the students reported their success in overcoming problems of understanding, reading, listening and speaking the host country language, such as:

"... to understand the host country people, since I did not know any word in that language at the beginning" (male French student who was in Greece).

"... to master German - I stayed for a month in Ludwigshafen before I actually started studying in Freiburg. I worked at ...(X Company) in a laboratory which I found extremely difficult at times but after a month I had learned more German than I had in the last 2 years at university" (female British student who was in Germany).

"... to write a summary of a thick book in the host country language" (male Belgian student who was in Italy).

As already mentioned above, successful solutions to accommodation problems were referred to by about 10 percent of the ERASMUS students.

As the responses to the open questions were difficult to quantify, the subsequent impressions have to be presented with some caution. It seems to us, however, justified to point to attitudes expressed in responses to open questions which differed according to home country.

French students were most often intrigued by academic experiences abroad. They referred most often to academic issues in describing their most positive experiences as well as the most difficult thing they successfully accomplished.

English and Irish students referred extensively to cultural experiences and to personal contacts established during the study abroad period. They considered the ERASMUS supported period abroad most valuable regarding their own personality development.

German students mentioned academic and cultural experiences frequently, but they often compared the host country most unfavourably with their home country, sometimes referring to every-day matters such as standards of sanitation.

Dutch students most often seemed to be dissatisfied with their experiences abroad. As the replies to the closed questions discussed above show, they were not dissatisfied in general, but a not insignificant number of Dutch students expressed their dissatisfaction with various issues, such as administrative problems abroad.

Students from most southern European countries, though mentioning various problems faced in the host country, by and large described the study abroad period most favourably. A sizeable number explicitly asked us to make their gratitude known for having had this opportunity to study abroad within the framework of the ERASMUS programme.

10.4 Desired Duration of the ERASMUS Supported Period

Both the positive experiences during the study abroad period and the limits of what they could experience and achieve during their stay led many students to wish for a longer stay abroad than initially intended or supported.

Of all the ERASMUS students, 68 percent stated that they would have liked to spend a longer period abroad. Those who wished for an additional period abroad would have liked to stay an additional 8.3 months on average (an average of 5.5 months for all ERASMUS students).

As reported in Chapter 3, the ERASMUS students responding to the questionnaire had spent an average of 7.1 months abroad supported by the ERASMUS programme. Given their additional desirable duration, the average duration would then be 12.6 months.

27 percent did achieve an extension of the stay abroad by 5.9 months by other means. This extension corresponds to 1.5 months extension on average for all ERASMUS students.

It might be added that some Inter-University Cooperation Programmes requiring more than one year abroad actually applied for a second phase of support for their students and were in some cases awarded this. According to the information provided in Chapter 3, six percent of the students stayed abroad for more than one year with ERASMUS support.

Table 10.5
Desired Duration of Extension of Period Abroad, by Country of Home University
(mean)

	B	D	DK	E	F	GR	I	IRL	NL	P	UK	Total
				Country of home university								Total
Number of Months	5.8	8.7	6.0	7.7	8.5	13.9	10.7	6.3	5.1	14.3	8.4	8.4
(n)	(138)	(476)	(31)	(226)	(416)	(29)	(214)	(24)	(84)	(7)	(401)	2046

Question 7.1: Would you have liked to spend a longer period abroad?

Table 10.6
Duration of Realized Extension of Period Abroad, by Country of Home
University (mean)

	Country of home university											Total
	B	D	DK	E	F	GR	I	IRL	NL	P	UK	
Number of Months	9.5	4.8	3.0	5.5	6.2	5.6	8.7	4.5	3.3	3.0	3.1	5.9
(n)	(15)	(146)	(5)	(59)	(190)	(7)	(207)	(4)	(18)	(1)	(155)	(807)

7.2: Did you extend your study period abroad beyond the period supported by your ERASMUS mobility grant, i.e. by means of financial support from sources other than ERASMUS? If yes, by how many months?

11. Determinants of Academic Progress Abroad and Recognition

A statistical analysis was undertaken designed to identify some of the key determinants of academic success of the study period abroad supported by the ERASMUS scheme. Regression and variance analysis was employed in examining the possible impact of personal background variables, major study profile data, academic preparation, assistance and guidance abroad, various academic issues abroad and finally, problems experienced during the study period abroad concerning the academic progress as well as the extent of recognition granted. As the possible factors included determine the extent of prolongation of study more strongly than the extent of recognition granted for courses actually taken, the degree of correspondence between the courses actually recognized, and the typical study load for a corresponding period at home, the findings regarding the two latter measures of recognition are not presented here.

As Charts 11.1 and 11.2 show, personal background data (age, gender and parental educational background) hardly played any role in explaining the perceived academic progress abroad in comparison with academic progress during a corresponding period at home, or in explaining the extent of prolongation of the overall study period due to the study abroad period. As regards the profile of the ICP or the study programme, academic progress abroad and (non-) prolongation was much more clearly linked to the country of the home institution than to the host country, the field of study, the duration of the study period abroad or the timing of the study period abroad within the overall course programme.

Chart 11.1
Determinants of Academic Progress Abroad

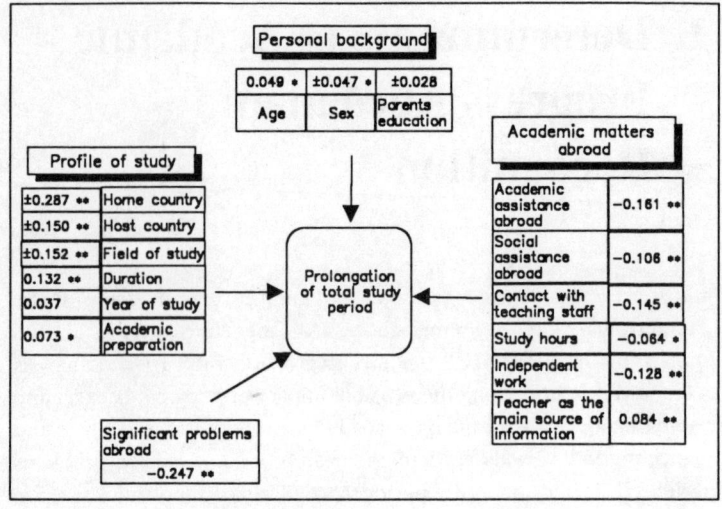

Chart 11.2
Determinants of Prolongation of Total Study Period

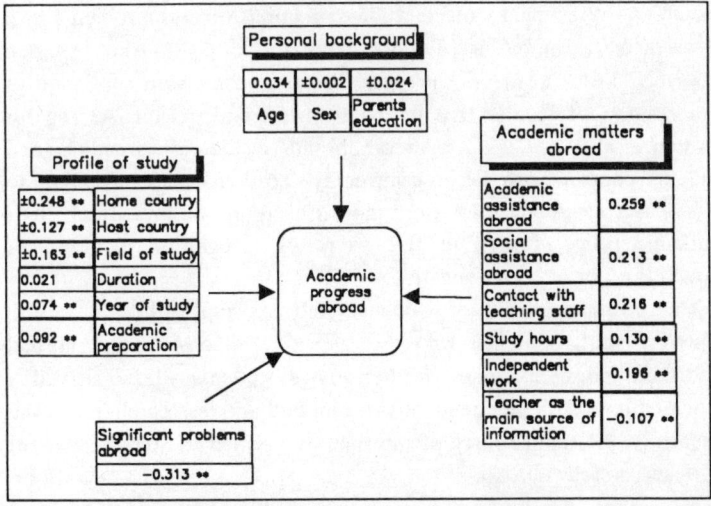

As regards the students' experiences and activities abroad, we note a stronger link between the possible factors observed to the - self-reported - academic progress abroad than to any of the measures of recognition chosen. As one might expect, students naming various problems they experienced at home were most likely to be those who reported relatively little academic progress abroad and who expected a prolongation of studies due to the study abroad period. As regards assistance and academic matters abroad, academic assistance and students' contacts with the host university's academic staff turned out to be key factors. Again, they were more closely linked to self-perceived academic progress than to the extent of recognition in terms of expecting no or little prolongation.

The positive impact of guidance and assistance did not mean, however, that students who experienced "spoon-feeding" abroad reported highest successes. Rather, those students who observed a strong emphasis on independent study abroad and less emphasis on the teacher as the main source of information seemed to study somewhat more successfully abroad.

Altogether, the findings suggest that study conditions at the host institution for the ERASMUS students played a role in shaping progress during the study abroad period and in ensuring academic recognition upon return. There was not, however, any single key factor which could be viewed as the major starting point for improvements. Finally, the differences of academic achievement by home country also suggest that academic preparation at the home institution was a contributing factor in the amount of academic success achieved during the study period abroad.

Chapter 12

Summary

The study reports the major findings of the questionnaire survey "Experiences of ERASMUS Students 1988/89". Students awarded a grant by the Commission of the European Communities to spend a period of about 3 to 12 months at an institution of higher education in another EC Member State were asked to provide information about their educational biography, the preparation for and their experiences during the study period abroad, and the outcomes in terms of recognition, academic progress, foreign language proficiency, knowledge and opinions of culture and society of the host country, etc. The ERASMUS Programme was inaugurated in 1987/88 and this first survey, aimed to be repeated biennially, addressed the second cohort of ERASMUS students: 3 212 students provided valid responses a few months after the study period abroad in the academic year 1988/89.

Altogether, about 11 000 students were awarded an ERASMUS grant in 1988/89. About 5 000 - all whose addresses were made available by the programme coordinators of their home departments - were sent a questionnaire; the response rate was 67 percent. Among the respondents, some countries, as well as those students staying abroad for more than half a year were overrepresented. In statistically adjusting the responses to the profile of all students, however, it appeared that the responses were only marginally affected by differences in the response rates.

The major findings of the study are summarized below. Some of them certainly challenge widespread views about the strengths and weaknesses of study in other countries of the European Community in the framework of the ERASMUS programme.

As regards the *profile of the participating students*, a wide range of fields of study was supported by ERASMUS grants. On average, students were older than 23 years and had completed 2.7 years of study before they went abroad. They spent seven months on average in the host country, and 22 percent of them participated in a work placement while abroad.

54 percent of the ERASMUS-supported students surveyed were female. 37 percent reported that their father, their mother, or both of them were college-trained. Most students had spent some period abroad prior to the ERASMUS-supported study period.

We note that participating departments had developed a substantial range of provisions for *preparation* of their own students for study abroad as well as providing administrative and academic advice and support for incoming ERASMUS students from other EC countries during the study period abroad. For example, 51 percent of the students participated in mandatory preparatory courses, and only five went to the host university without any specific preparation. Only 13 percent reported no support in administrative and organisational issues (registration, course selection, accommodation etc.) by the host institution of higher education, and only 11 percent were not given guidance and advice in academic matters. On average, however, students assessed these measures prior to and during the study period abroad somewhat cautiously. Obviously, many of them expected some improvement in these areas.

In most of the topics addressed, striking differences can be observed according to country, be it the country of the home institution of higher education or the host country. By and large, *conditions and provisions for study abroad* varied more strongly by country than by disciplinary cultures and conditions. For example, the proportion of students reporting no organised preparation ranged, according to home country, from 13 to 88 percent. Serious academic problems were mentioned, depending on host country, by at least seven percent and at most 23 percent of the students. No support in finding accommodation was reported by seven percent of the students hosted in the country in which most support was provided, and by 27 percent of the students hosted in the country in which support was least common. Finally, less academic progress abroad than at home was reported between three percent and 26 percent of the ERASMUS students.

There seemed to be a North-South discrepancy: students from northern countries in the European Community tended to rate their study environment at home relatively positively and assessed the conditions for study in the southern host countries less favourably; students from southern European countries rated their study conditions and experiences abroad during the ERASMUS-supported period more favourably.

Most ERASMUS students had a broad range of *academic, cultural and social experiences in the host country.* About two-thirds frequently visited museums or attended concerts, theatre, cinema, etc. while 61 percent reported frequent contact with the teaching staff of the host institution of higher education. More than two-thirds took courses involving content not available at the home institution, and more than half experienced new methods of teaching and learning. About 90 percent of the students took, at least in part, courses taught in the language of the host country. Students spent on average 17 hours weekly in taking lectures - about three hours less than at home.

There is no single item among the *problems faced during the study period abroad* which was considered to be extremely serious by the ERASMUS students. For example, in response to a list of 19 possible problems, nine problems were often (between 26 and 15 %) rated as relatively serious. Among them, too much contact with people from home country (26 %), accommodation (22 %), and financial matters (21 %) were stated most frequently, but academic problems abroad were reported almost as often, notably differences between home and host country regarding teaching and learning styles (17 %) and taking examinations in a foreign language (15 %).

On the basis of recent public debates, one might have expected that *accommodation* stood out as the most serious problem and, in fact, students mentioned accommodation issues most frequently in response to an open question regarding major problems. According to the responses referred to above, however, it is only one of three major problems, with 18 percent of the ERASMUS students not provided with any help in finding accommodation. On average students spent only about 10 hours in finding accommodation abroad while 22 percent rated the quality of accommodation as bad.

As regards *financial issues*, one should bear in mind that the ERASMUS Programme aims to provide means for the additional costs incurred by studying in another Member State of the European Community, notably roundtrip fare, additional living expenses and possibly costs of language training. On average, students surveyed were awarded about ECU 1 100 for an average period of slightly more than seven months, i.e. ECU 158 per month. Based in part on detailed students' responses and in part on estimates, we conclude that students spent on average per month about ECU 65 for additional living costs, ECU 30 for the roundtrip fare, ECU 40 for retaining their home accommodation, and a further 10 ECU for additional tuition and fees. We estimate that the ERASMUS grants in 1988/89 on average covered the additional costs for study abroad. This does not exclude, however, financial constraints: some students reported much higher costs abroad than support received (whereas the opposite was true for others); 21 percent of the students reported that they experienced serious financial problems. The data did not reveal how many students lived more thriftily abroad than at home and how many students did not go abroad because they considered the support as being too low.

On the basis of prior research we developed three criteria for *recognition*:

(a) Degree of recognition: 77 percent of the study actually undertaken abroad was recognized, and 68 percent of the ERASMUS students reported full recognition according to this measure.

(b) Degree of correspondence: According to this measure, recognition corresponded on average to 73 percent of typical study at home, whereby only 40 percent of the students reported complete recognition in this respect. As students took 17 percent less courses abroad on average than usual at home, we might consider the 'degree of correspondence' as relatively high in comparison to the 'degree of recognition'.

(c) Degree of non-prolongation: Finally, many ERASMUS students assumed that their study in another EC country would lead to a prolongation of study. If non-prolongation is the measure of complete recognition, only 47 percent of study abroad during an ERASMUS-supported period was recognized, while 56 percent of students did not expect any prolongation.

Recognition of study abroad was unlikely to be recognized completely for all students, because some students took fewer courses, failed some courses or deliberately chose courses not fitting their home curricula in order to broaden their horizons. This notwithstanding, the findings of the survey suggest that the idea of the ERASMUS programme according to which participating departments grant recognition as a rule, was not (yet) fully implemented.

In contrast, students themselves rated their *academic progress abroad* very positively. 55 percent considered their academic progress abroad better, and only 19 percent reported less academic progress than during a respective period at home. Even allowing for some overestimation on the part of the students, these findings suggest that there is more academic value to study abroad as judged by the students' themselves than is formally recognized by the home institutions of higher education.

ERASMUS students acquired substantial *knowledge of their host country*, but their *opinions* on the host country on average did not change substantially. (Attitudes to a host country, to international relations etc. might possibly change in longer cycles than study abroad periods lasting a few months or even a year). Opinions about higher education of the respective home and host country indicated an north-south gap: by and large, students from southern EC Member States rated higher education in the host country more favourably than higher education at home, whereas the reverse is true for students from northern EC Member States.

Almost all students considered a study period in another EC country as an academically and culturally worthwhile experience. Cultural and linguistic outcomes were more positively assessed than academic outcomes. In response to open questions, many indicated that they highly appreciated the opportunity to get acquainted with people from the host country and other countries, and to get to know the life, the culture and society of the host country. As regards 'worst things' experienced, problems of accommodation stood out, but concerns expressed about crime (by 7 %) and negative characteristics of the host country and the people (stated by 5 %) were not completely trivial. Many students considered successful study in a foreign language and foreign higher education environment as the most 'challenging' experience in the host country.

Any evaluative judgement about the findings faces the problems of setting criteria. For example, is 90 percent recognition expected, and thus 80 percent recognition an indicator of substantial problems and of a need for improvement of the various measure aimed to ensure recognition? Or is 75 percent recognition expected as a rule in the face of 'unavoidable' problems of learning in a foreign language, adaptation to a foreign culture and the desire to make use of the period abroad for extra-curricular experiences? In our analyses, we compared the findings with those of a survey conducted in the mid-eighties of students participating in relatively well-established study abroad programmes in the United Kingdom, France, the Federal Republic of Germany, Sweden and the United States. We note that ERASMUS students reported very similar study activities abroad, a very similar assessment of their experiences abroad, slightly more problems and slightly less recognition. In taking into consideration, however, that a substantial proportion of cooperation and student exchange was newly established in order to be awarded ERASMUS support, we conclude that the ERASMUS programme was rapidly successful, as far as the experiences of the second cohort of ERASMUS students was concerned.

Many commentators have noted that the ERASMUS programme could be more valuable if more funds were available, if administrative processes were improved, most notably in transferring student mobility grants to the students more quickly, and if some conditions for study abroad - notably accommodation - were more favourable. The ERASMUS students themselves pointed out that improvements were also desirable in other areas, notably the quality of preparation, the extent and quality of advice and support at the host institution and, above all, in recognition, i.e. issues for which the institutions of higher education and their departments are not only predominantly responsible, but have also, in their applications to the ERASMUS programme, undertaken to resolve.

ERASMUS Monographs

1. **Student Mobility within ERASMUS 1987/88 - A Statistical Survey**

   U. Teichler, F. Maiworm, W. Steube
   Arbeitspapiere, 24, Wissenschaftliches Zentrum für Berufs- und Hochschulforschung, Kassel 1990

   Contact:
   Prof. Ulrich TEICHLER, Wissenschaftliches Zentrum für Berufs- und Hochschulforschung, Gesamthochschule Kassel, Henschelstraße 4, D-3500 Kassel, Tel.: 49-561-804 2415, Fax: 49-561-804 3301

2. **L'amélioration de la préparation linguistique et socioculturelle des étudiants ERASMUS**

   G. Baumgratz-Gangl, N. Deyson, G. Kloss
   Unité langues pour la Coopération en Europe (ULCE) auprès du Centre d'Information et de Recherche sur l'Allemagne Contemporaine (CIRAC), July 1989.

   Contact:
   Dr. Gisela BAUMGRATZ-GANGL, Unité langues pour la coopération en Europe (ULCE), Institut européen d'éducation et de politique sociale, c/o Université de Paris IX-Dauphine, Place du Maréchal de Lattre de Tassigny, F-75116 Paris; Tel.: 33-1-47.27.06.41 / 45.05.14.10, poste 3000, Fax: 33-1-45.53.81.34

3. **Recognition: A Typological Overview of Recognition Issues within ERASMUS**

   U. Teichler
   Werkstattberichte, 29, Wissenschaftliches Zentrum für Berufs- und Hochschulforschung, Kassel 1990

   Contact:
   Prof. Ulrich TEICHLER, cf. Monograph 1

4. **Untersuchung über die Beteiligung der Medizin im ERASMUS-Programm (Study on the Participation of Medicine in ERASMUS)**
   In German with an English summary
   K. Schnitzer, E. Korte
   HIS Hochschulplanung 85, HIS Hochschul-Informations-System GmbH, Hannover 1990

   Contact:
   Dr. Klaus SCHNITZER, HIS Hochschul-Informations-System, Postfach 2920, D-3000 Hannover; Tel.: 49-511-1220297 / Fax: 49-511-1220250

5. **Teacher Education and the ERASMUS Programme**
   M. Bruce
   In: **European Journal of Teacher Education**, Vol. 12, No. 3, 1989
   (pp. 197 - 228) ISSN 0261-9768 - Brussels 1989

   Contact:
   A.T.E.E. - Association for Teacher Education in Europe, Rue de
   la Concorde 51, B-1050 Bruxelles. Tel.: 32-2-512 1734 / Fax: 32-2-512 3265

6. **Les obstacles à la participation au programme ERASMUS dans le domaine de l'art et du design**
   P. Kuentz
   Strasbourg, July 1989.

   Contact:
   Prof. Pierre KUENTZ, Ecole des Arts Decoratifs, 1 rue de l'Académie, F-6700 Strasbourg; Tel.: 33-88-353858

7. **ERASMUS et les arts du spectacle (musique, théâtre, danse)**
   D. Barriolade
   EUROCREATION, Paris, July 1989.

   Contact:
   Directeur de Projets Denise Barriolade, EUROCREATION, L'agence française des jeunes créateurs européens, 3 rue Debelleyme, F-75003 Paris; Tel.: 33-1-48047879 / Fax: 33-1-40299246

8. Comparative Evaluation of ERASMUS ICPs in the Subject Areas of Business Management, Chemistry, History

Prof. A. Monasta

Università di Firenze, July 1989

Contact:
Prof. Attilio MONASTA, Università degli Studi di Firenze, Facoltà di Magistero, Dipartemento di Scienze dell' Educazione, Via Cavour, 82, I-50129 Firenze; Tel.: 39-55-2757751/2757761

9. Survey of Academic Recognition within the Framework of ICPs in the Field of Mechanical Engineering

H. Risvig Henriksen

SEFI (Société Européenne pour la Formation des Ingénieurs), Bruxelles, August 1989

Contact:
S.E.F.I. - Société Européenne pour la Formation des Ingénieurs, Rue de la Concorde 51, B-1050 Bruxelles; Tel.: 32-2-512 1734 / Fax: 32-2-512 3265

10. ERASMUS PROGRAMME - Report on the Experience Acquired in the Application of the ERASMUS Programme 1987-1989

Commission of the European Communities, SEC(89) 2051
Brussels, 13 December 1989

Contact:
ERASMUS Bureau, cf. Monograph 2

11. La coopération inter-universitaire dans les sciences agronomiques, ERASMUS 1978/88 - 1990/91

Philippe Ruffio

ENSAR, Départment des Sciences économiques et sociales, June 1990

Contact:
ERASMUS Bureau, cf. Monograph 2

12. Student Mobility 1988/89 - A Statistical Survey

U. Teichler, R. Kreitz, F. Maiworm

Arbeitspapiere, 26, Wissenschaftliches Zentrum für Berufs- und Hochschulforschung, Kassel 1991

<u>Contact:</u>
Prof. Ulrich TEICHLER, cf. Monograph 1

13. Experience of ERASMUS Students 1988/89

U. Teichler

Werkstattberichte, 32, Wissenschaftliches Zentrum für Berufs- und Hochschulforschung, Kassel 1991

<u>Contact:</u>
Prof. Ulrich TEICHLER, cf. Monograph 1

14. Learning in Europe: The ERASMUS Experience

F. Maiworm, W. Steube, U. Teichler

Jessica Kingsley Publishers, London 1991 (£ 18.-)

<u>Contact:</u>
Jessica Kingsley Publishers, 118 Pentonville Road, UK-London N1 9JN; Tel.: 44-71833 2307 / Fax 44-71-837 2917

Index